ELEMENTS OF THE FREE DANCE

BY

ELIZABETH SELDEN

NEW YORK

A. S. BARNES AND COMPANY

INCORPORATED

1930

THIS BOOK IS DEDICATED
TO THE CAUSE OF STUDY AND CRITICISM
OF THE FREE DANCE

CONTENTS

CONTENTS

FOREWORD

Barefoot dancing, which has been practiced now for a quarter of a century, is still known only through comparison with the ballet, and has never attempted identification by its own right. Somewhat awed by the strongly entrenched position of this older sister of hers, barefoot dancing has, at least in America, lived under the shadow of that strong fortress. The name, the whole terminology of barefoot dancing, is still an uncertain and hardly enough debated topic, and this is the more astonishing as the actual practice of it has long proven its worth and has certainly come to stay, not only for the present but for some time in the future. With the advent of barefoot dancing, the Dance has once more advanced to the rank of an educational subject, which had not been the case for some centuries; and it will lie with the dancers themselves to establish it as an art.

We are suffering from a lack of clearly recognized delimitations on the one hand, and on the other, there is apparently no unified front with respect to aims, nor a common basis of technique. This state of affairs will continue until an integration of terminology shall prove that anything can be straightened out which can be talked about; then it will soon be apparent that the dividing lines have, after all, been few, and that we have all had much more of a common procedure than we ever knew we had in the days when an exaggerated individualism barred the door to understanding.

For the present, each studio still practices a method and a terminology possibly characteristic of itself, but hardly understandable outside of its narrow precincts; and students are very seldom encouraged to acquaint themselves with the great world of unknown quantities on the outside. Nor are they, for the most part, accustomed to comparing and analyzing even leading forms of the Dance. The inference is clear, and cannot help the cause of the Dance; behind so much exclusiveness, the public suspects that there are rather narrow limitations, and this practice has also left the impression that the Free Dance * is hardly an organized art, and is bound to remain a field of endless

* See Glossary of Terms.

[viii]

experimentation. On the whole, our public has had scant sources of information, as compared with the other arts, and with dance literature in other countries. We have seen a few textbooks come out, it is true, outlining some individual method for the public, and some, which were dwelling especially on the educational aspect of the Dance. It is also characteristic of this state of things that we have had to wait until 1928 for the first word on the barefoot dance from its great pioneer, Isadora Duncan.

In the meanwhile, the time seems to have become ripe for a synthesis, and the main obstacle is doubtless the lack of a professional terminology.

This little book is offered as a first step in this direction. Can we not focus the attention of students and teachers alike on the possibilities of some sort of synthesis * which may be used as a working basis for most types of barefoot dancing? In the common cause of the Free Dance, I should like to invite research and investigation of the whole territory it has so far covered.

Such a study as this is of necessity brief; the re-

* Not necessarily the one offered here—which was written rather as a general impression *of states and stages of the past than with a view to outlining the future.*

sults have been arrived at through much analysis, years of observation and comparison of European and American modes of dancing, and by a process of elimination rather than by elaboration. Of principles that would be acceptable to so many different methods, there can be but few.

However, there are—or should be—some minimum requirements common to all. In the search for that which binds together, I have dealt at some length with these. In order to avoid duplication, much had to be discarded, especially the temptation to dwell upon technique—which would amount to outlining one's own. This book could not make itself the advocate of any particular form or method of the Dance, let alone my own.

It seemed a waste of effort to enlarge upon topics which have been very successfully dealt with elsewhere, as for instance, Music with relation to the Dance (see Dalcroze: *Rhythm, Music,* and *Education*); likewise questions which constitute a topic in themselves and are somewhat apart from a general discussion, such as: Composition in its larger aspect, the Dance without Music, the Dance Script, etc.

Several of these topics have had to receive their

only mention in the Glossary which intends to be a small contribution to the burning question of terminology. It purports to give a clarification of already existing terms with which the lay public may not be familiar, and introduces a few new ones. Only in a few instances suggestions for substitutions or for elimination have been made. I feel very strongly that we can gain nothing by going back to the French terminology peculiar to the ballet. The motions of the New Dance, although sometimes almost identical with the older forms, have been for the most part discovered, or, if you will, rediscovered by way of an entirely new experience which formed them, or transformed them, out of the substance of our age. The old French terms remind us of a dangerous affectation—the twentieth century thinking and feeling in terms of Louis Quatorze sophistications! Esperanto might express us more adequately to-day.

Our language must clothe what our spirit has formed. We may learn from others, but it is not necessary for us to-day to establish at once an international code of dancing terms, desirable though it may seem. We can trust the development of technical terms for the dance to happen in the same way as it has in other arts: by slow accretion, and by contributions from many sources. It is usually the nation that has made the strongest contribution to an art at some significant point of development which leaves an undeniable mark on its terminology. Italy has thus put her stamp on music, France, upon modern painting, and it is possible that Germany will do it for the New Dance.

What nobody has given us yet, though, is a satisfactory collective term for that new dispensation of the Dance which I reckon as having begun with Isadora's first pilgrimage to Europe in 1905, when she took her message to Europe, having failed to arouse her homeland. She herself once speaks of the "New Dance." * I have long leaned toward the expression "The New Dance" which has been much used in Europe. But aside from the fact that a new thing cannot remain new forever, the term does not recommend itself for other reasons. It seems that it has already changed in meaning. It begins to be more particularly applied to the new turn which the Dance has

* "To find those primary movements for the human body from which shall evolve the movement of the future Dance in ever varying natural, unending sequences, that is the duty of the new Dance of to-day."

taken in Germany as a consequence of the combined efforts of Rudolf von Laban and Mary Wigman. And there it now rightly belongs—if they want to accept it. These pioneers turned a corner in 1914 with which they have initiated the second phase of what I call the "Free Dance," until a better term can be found. The Dance of the twentieth century was begotten by a call for freedom; and it is still struggling both for and under this fine heritage.

A chapter which presented itself more as a necessity than from choice, was the comparison between the Free Dance and the Ballet. It was not my desire to conduct this investigation along the lines of opposition to the ballet but we are as yet so close to the old order that the antithesis is inevitable. Proof of it is the standing question: "What is the difference between this form of dancing and the Ballet?" which every dancing teacher has heard a thousand times. In a quarter of a century, we shall no longer speak of the New Dance, but of Our Dance, the Dance simply; as of our own times, incontestably in possession of its rightful heritage—public interest. Then shall come the better comparisons—comparisons between different stages of its own kind, just as we have ceased to see modern painting on the background of the academic pallor of 1850, but begin the count with the new generations of the post-impressionists, cubists, expressionists, futurists, and so on—when we want to establish the place and the meaning for a painting of to-day.

In another quarter of a century, when the forms of the Free Dance shall have become somewhat integrated and a terminology established, it may be interesting to compare that advanced stage of progress with the results of the first twenty-five years, when the elements of the Free Dance appeared as yet loosely connected—flotsam and jetsam from the great deep of that ever-appearing consciousness, that can no more exhaust itself in one form of art alone than it can halt for centuries on one point of artistic perfection, be that perfection ever so great.

I am deeply indebted to Miss Sarah N. Cleghorn for her expert advice in connection with this manuscript, and for her advance criticism. She tendered a much-needed encouragement to the faltering (literary) conscience of one not native with the language, whose real profession is the Dance. If I dared to overcome this double handicap, and turn to writing, it was out of interest for the Dance. This is the book which nobody would write for me when I needed it, in my training years, and I offer it with all the hesitancy attending a venture along untrodden paths.

ELIZABETH S. SELDEN.

UNCASVILLE, CONNECTICUT,
April, 1930

Part I

THE INNER NECESSITY

The student of barefoot dancing is often bewildered when he finds himself confronted by a maze of different names seemingly all attached to types of barefoot dancing of a kindred variety. There is Rhythmic Dancing and Interpretative Dancing; Nature Dancing and Natural Dancing; Art-Dance and the Dance-as-an-Art; Expression Dancing; Expressionistic Dancing; the Absolute Dance of Germany; and a multitude of "systems" and "methods" attached to individual names.

To classify these unknown quantities correctly—if such a thing can be done to-day—is not half as important as to be acquainted with their common denominator.

What is the essence of barefoot dancing? Evidently it is not the lack of shoes, although this negative statement expresses an attitude which contains a very positive challenge to the symbol of an old, worn-out order. Symbolically, the shoe stands for repression. Practically, it stands for something superfluous—it is not the shoe that dances, but the foot inside. And that foot inside a ballet slipper is most of the time so completely ruined by the encasement, that famous toe-dancers could not stand an inspection of the very part of their body to which they owe, so to speak, their existence. The ballet shoe belongs to the epoch of the hoop-skirt and the pinched waist. Nothing seems more natural to-day than that this old order, an order which had held sway for an incredibly long time,* should give way before the vigorous protests of a new race of women. They had become conscious of their freedom and of their opportunities in the struggle for emancipation which marked the beginning of the twentieth century. When Isadora Duncan first danced without shoes, she rendered the Dance a service which should never be forgotten. Her genius had seen the inevitable. To-day, hundreds of thousands of women are barefoot dancers. The simple fact is that when a new order was breaking everywhere, the time was ripe for a new spirit also in the Dance.

Given the fact that we have attained a new order of dancing in the barefoot dance, the question re-

* The beginnings of the Ballet go back to the sixteenth century at least. See Glossary.

[4]

turns: what is the common link between all these different methods which have sprung up in the pursuit of a new ideal? What is the nature of the inner necessity which the barefoot dancer follows in choosing his means and technique of outward expression, and how are they dependent upon one another?

For the purpose of extracting the essence which all these many offshoots of the same ideal have in common, we will speak of these different types together: as the Free Dance, and examine aspects which set this mode of dancing aside as something definitely recognizable, radically different from older types of dancing: Ballet, Folk and National dancing.

The Dance shares with all art the aim of projecting an inner vision into the world without. The Dance does it through visible motion, and partakes at once of the three realms: Time, Space, Thought. If the older forms of dancing contented themselves with an existence which was more or less circumscribed by time and space, the New Dance dwells besides very definitely on thought and feeling.

It is the new demand.

True, any form of dancing demands it, inasmuch as the mere counting of steps, or the distribution of space patterns, requires some mental action, but this belongs in a far greater degree to the exigencies of the Free Dance. We can imagine a dance composition of the new order carried out almost in place, making little or nothing of the floor pattern; but it is perfectly unthinkable that the *idea* should be missing. An able dancer may execute his idea with a minimum of motion. He may even retard the progression of motion to immobility, but unless he has made evident the progression of thought or emotion which commanded, as a final consummation, this immobility, and unless he can fill this immobility with life-giving force, which in turn lays hold upon his audience, then his dance has failed.

It would be possible for a toe-dancer to carry out a little dance or series of steps almost unthinking, quite mechanically, after once having learned it.* It has become for him a matter of routine, and he may even be proud of the fact; his education consists of reducing his body to the uncomplaining state of an infallible instrument. Thought processes have been almost eliminated in favor of a quick succession of actions from motor muscles working almost automatically.

For the interpretative, or expression-dancer to do the same would be out of the question; he would look impossibly silly. Thought is the rein which he cannot let go of for an instant, without becoming incompe-

---

* To all outward appearances, the mechanistic dances which have recently come in use as "fillers" on dance programs, would belong in the same category. However, the act of reducing the naturally flowing lines of the human body to the level of a machine, can only be the product of an almost painful mental effort. More artful than soulful, these often very amusing exhibitions of skill suffer, if anything, from too much intellectualism.

tent, or a pretender; an incompetent, who passes beauty, music, and emotion by and knows it not; or worse still: has killed it, if he was a pretender.

This thought-action appears from the earliest stages of apprenticeship in the Dance. At first, it takes the form of a constant necessity for guiding and selecting the motion; it might be termed a process of measuring one's individual capacities. It is a listening to the inner and outer self, a studying of the velocity and the degree in which the latter carries out the commands of the former in coördination and muscular control. It is a growing knowledge of the secret place where force and lightness meet to balance each other.

There is no essential difference between this and the start in other forms of dancing. However, the experience of ballet, folk or national dancing is limited by a rather different absolute demand: that of form, not of *some* form, *any* form that recommends itself to the artistic sense, but of a pattern of fixed outline. You may go so far only, you *must* go so far; but no farther. Apparently, there is no room for individual research and creative exuberance—at least not for the pupil, although the master may reach this point. A movement is classified as beautiful or not, according as it is executed, correctly or incorrectly, following the code, or departing from it; and a "beautiful" movement is alike beautiful for all.

The New Dancer must know his limitations and possibilities in a different sense. *He must feel harmony of line for himself,* and must know space composition to the extent where he can compose his own movements, or else adapt the model of motion before him to the proportions of his body. An exercise, carried out beautifully by one person, may not produce the same effect in another, although he, too, may have experienced fully the even flow of motion and emotion; may have timed himself exactly and otherwise obeyed the pattern. This, in itself, is doing much. If in spite of this, he has not attained at a result satisfactory to the eye, the fault lies usually with the proportions of his body, and he will have to amend the motion accordingly.*

What then, in the face of these subtle requirements,

* This, however, is a subtle question, and belongs properly to the latter stages of training. While yet in training, the pupils' body changes constantly. Glaring disproportions, it is true, cannot be obliterated altogether, but it often happens that the right training will result in bringing the body into much better proportions. At this stage the master's lead is the best mirror.

should be the fate of the "poor" pupil, the untalented or shy person who has taken up the Free Dance in good faith and in the hope of some results? Is he condemned to making a fool of himself? In no wise, if he is sincerely striving. Just because the right thought—qualities of intelligence, concentration, attention, understanding, and education—enters so largely into this art, it can hold possibilities for so many people who might fail in other lines of dancing which stress only the physical development of the dancer and leave his mental assets largely unused. Once in a while, these possibilities might even lead up to professional proficiency for some pupil who seemed unpromising at the start. At any rate, the large class of amateurs—sincere lovers of the Dance, who enjoy it quite aside from professional ambitions, —usually find their right field of endeavor in the Free Dance because it will take into account the development of the whole personality.

Professional students of the Free Dance, however, will do well to understand the unshakable fact: that physical fitness is the first, and by far the most important, factor in the making of a dancer. If there has been in the past a tendency among adherents of the Free Dance to doubt or overlook that inexorable demand, the development of the last ten years has, at least in Europe, completely turned the scales in favor of the new dancers. In amount of skill and work, these new dancers are often overtaking their brethren from the ballet. They have found that mental qualifications alone cannot produce a professional. Mental qualifications may help the understanding of the Dance, they are most important, indeed, for the shaping of it, but the utmost mental effort and striving alone will not suffice. One must be born for the Dance, as one is born a painter, or a musician.

The thought-element in the New Dance may thus become a help to some; to many, who cannot fulfill its requirement, it is an absolute bar (and that is well—for without a natural process of selection, would art remain art very long?); and alas! this thought, falsely understood, has also become the large gate by which erroneous conceptions, and a never-ending stream of would-be-professionals have entered the field. Thousands of enthusiasts who afterwards become the unwitting accusers against the art they poorly practice, stream yearly through this gate which to them is the open sesame to an indiscriminate pil-

[11]

fering of beauty, a glorious indulging in sentimentality, or simply, an antidote for undefinable restlessness. They may have intelligence.—Yes, but more
is needed. *Much* intelligence, and even more;
thought! Deep. Laborious. Creative thought.
They offer sentiment.—Yes, art needs sentiment, if
sentiment means feeling; at any rate sentiment does
not mean sentimentality, nor does emotional striving
alone beget art.

Better no thought at all, than thought without depth,
background or direction. Shallow thought is the
worst foe of art. It may arrive at creating a semblance of the real thing, and give out that semblance
for the thing which had better not be called to life
than be held up by artificial means.—There is no
room in art for hazy thinking. Hardly is there a
worse crime for any teacher than to keep his pupils
in a state of mental dependence upon him, or to allow
them to indulge in an atmosphere of soft somnolence.
All vague notions must fall before a pupil can call
himself a master. The moment comes when he is
alone with himself. Now he must create. For many
there now begins a frantic search for the things that
are. As if *creating* did not mean bringing up from

the bottom of the soul the things that *have not yet been*. They go to "find" what has already been enjoyed. Their own mind does not speak to them.—But the Dance is the silent language of the soul! What will you speak of, Dancers, if you cannot speak for yourselves?

This is where the new demand makes its second, definite selection. Let every apprentice, before he styles himself a master, spend two years alone, space and time before him. If, unafraid of what he has found then, he still persists with the Dance, the world will be richer for an artist.

What is the Free Dance?

A conquering of time and space through motion, which wells up from a deep inner necessity for unfoldment, and speaks, through the Dance, of that never-ending secret, that flow and ebb of life-force, which we call rhythm.   Our own rhythm; for there is also the rhythm of the machine which conquers space. The machine carries the rhythm of work; but when we dance, we are farthest removed from the machine. The rhythm of dancing is the rhythm of feast days, where we live, and give, of the superabundance of life.   In the Dance, we rest from work and enter into the feast chambers of human experience.

Many have said: the Dance is Life, but few know how deep this saying goes.   Life means, not only existence, being, momentary consciousness; if it is life, and not stagnation, it must mean change, transformation, progress, unfoldment.   *In this sense, the Dance is the most immediate,* and at the same time, the most abstract expression of Life.

The problem confronting the dancer, then, is not

[14]

merely the filling of time and space through motion
—machines could do that too. As an artist, the dancer
must *feel* time, love space, hear it talk to him as a
living presence full of untold possibilities; then he
may fill both with his dance,—an answer that is as
direct, beautiful, clear and moving—yes, possibly
more so—than any human tongue can ever make it.

The Dance has a thousand registers of expression.
It may become the most intimate song of the human
soul, expressing joy and laughter, sorrow and tears,
a sermon or a prayer, inaudible, yet comprehensible
to all. Here the dancer will *follow* in the lead of
rhythm, which reduces all his mental qualities, for the
time being, to a concentrated effort at listening within,
so as not to miss a shading of the eloquent voices of
which he has suddenly become the playmate, the vic-
tim, the translator and interpreter. It is a task which
can be done only with the utmost sincerity. Any effort
at pretense, any effort at sugar-coating his experience
by adding unnecessary prettiness, or any wincing
under its impact, will immediately betray itself.

Again, the dancer may concern himself primarily
with the artistic possibilities of space and time as
such, and, pushing rhythm before him in conscious

energy, give rein wholly to his fancy in heaping motion upon motion into space patterns, which pursue a rhythmic theme, either in music, or without musical accompaniment, to a conclusion. These dancers, the "pure motion" type, seem to be giving out of a superabundance of (physical as well as mental) life force, which, in by-gone centuries, might have found its fulfillment in some mighty epic.

Or the dancer may yield himself with all the wealth of his finely trained sensibilities to the impressions from a fixed theme, becoming a delicately vibrating instrument in the service of a thought, of a picture, or of another being; in short, using dramatization and impersonation.* There, the dancer gives himself up to some influence outside of himself, and consents to make this influence a part of his inner experience, translating it into gesture and dancing. As a ray of light, breaking through a prism, is not lost, engulfed, but emerges from the prism as light which has taken on a thousand colors, so the dramatic subject, handled by a dancer, does not lose its own character, but reappears again in motion, transformed by emotion.

These, then, are the possibilities which the dancer

* Forms of the applied or illustrative dance. See Glossary.

enjoys: he can yield to the thousand lyric tunes and modes of music, or he can listen solely to himself and his inner experience; he can design his dance for the sake of decorative effects—most symmetric dance patterns are of this nature—or evolve structural space compositions of a free type; he can consent to become the translator of dramatic feeling for himself or for others, and, if he is a genius, he can express a whole philosophy of life silently. This is the freedom which the Dance gives its followers. But the dancer can never leave the three realms which are given to him for an opportunity as well as for a limit of expression: time, space and thought. For instance, he cannot become a narrator—aim at the province of the spoken word. "Telling stories," however sweet, must be left to literature and the kindergarten of the Dance. The Dance as an art has nothing to do with it. If it would keep its essential nature, the Dance must remain a silent art. Its evolution as an independent art-form lies in this direction. The outward material of the Dance is motion. The dancer's dance is the music of his soul made visible; and motion, this mute, wonderful servant, becomes eloquent in the service of rhythm.

The language of the dancer must remain rhythm.
Language operates by means of parts of speech, of
which some fulfill a more important office while
others give a mere shading to the speech, lend color,
or serve as connecting or separating agents within a
group of words that gain in this way concise meaning. But leave out those connecting links, disturb
the order of the words, and they become incoherent,
can no longer be considered as speech. Language is
the ordering spirit which stands above, establishing
larger meaning by virtue of a right relationship among
the words. It is the master, ordering the words.

Rhythm is the artist, playing with the elements of
the Dance: movement, rest, force, balance, feeling,
intensity, line—which concurrently present the theme,
or idea, of a dance. The word rhythm belongs among
the most misunderstood and ill-used. Many speak
of it as if it were a synonym for "dance," others conceive of it as keeping time. The one idea is too
large, the other much too small.

Rhythm can never be the subject-matter of anything, not even of the Dance, *for it is an idea abstracted from two or more factors,* or the factor resulting from the comparison of them. It is always tied to the exteriorization of concrete values, without which it is unthinkable.

Sound-rhythms are tied to the concrete case when they have been produced by some instrument, or by some mechanical causes. The rhythm of the tom-tom is unthinkable without the tom-tom.

Linear rhythms are not felt without the illustration of concrete objects which exemplify them for the onlooker. In each case, the rhythm only becomes measurable, commits itself to the experience of the observer, when it is being actually produced, exteriorized, by some object which may be as elusive as water itself. For instance, whoever has once seen the wind play with the rippling waves, will forever after recognize the line of wave rhythm. But without this first experience, could one think of it?

Rhythm expresses itself as an ordering force not only in the Dance, in music and poetry, but in all art. It appears in the distribution of color and space in painting, plays an important part as form organization in sculpture and architecture.* There we have linear and spatial rhythm. It is an ordering, regulating quality in the distribution of sounds, lines, color, forms, words, and movement. *Rhythm expresses the relationship—in terms of time, space, or intensity,— of two or more concrete values which recur more than once. It is a feeling for, a measuring of intervals.* To feel rhythm is to have a sense for intervals.

---

* The distribution of columns in an arcade, for instance, presents a simple example of space composition, where the distance between the columns in its constantly recurring repetition of space pattern, is felt by the eye as a rhythmic experience.

MUSICAL RHYTHM It is in nowise necessary that these intervals recur at constantly even times or spaces. This is a popular fallacy induced by the "keeping time" idea. The development of music in the last two centuries has accustomed the ear to the beat of time, and the idea of a fixed meter has assumed the preponderance over the larger rhythms of the musical phrase, the theme, etc. Earlier music (as late as in the times of Bach) paid less respect to the principle of a fixed beat where the heaviness of the accent would lie on every first or third division of the bar; and modern composers are reverting to that conception.* Musical rhythm, then, implies the beat in music as well as those larger subdivisions along which the composer bids his themes to rise and to fall, the sound to swell or to diminish in intensity.

The whole matter or relationship of the component parts of any composition belongs to a feeling for

* As for instance, in syncopation. Syncopation is a means of circumventing the requirements of a fixed musical beat by shifting the accent. But many modern composers have completely overthrown the fixed meter; and we see any number of different meters used in the same composition, often without division into bars.

rhythm. Thus, rhythm becomes for the dancer a question far outreaching mere accuracy in keeping time with an accompanying instrument.* Rhythm orders the relation between the component parts of the dance, that is: movement, rest, force, feeling, intensity, line, besides establishing the measure, or wave length, so to speak, of the ever recurring pulsations within the larger whole. In this sense rhythm holds the balance for muscular tension and relaxation, for the rise and fall of visual movement, for the upstroke and down-stroke of the accent. These elementary rhythms must be known and felt, or gross mistakes would occur; but they can never be the end of the dance itself. They follow the law of technique: building up a trustworthy mechanism which must never be apparent as such, but will become entirely embodied in the pursuit of the larger aim. It will be useful to any dancer as a technician to know how to beat time, but the artist in him will not allow that knowledge to cut in on the smooth carrying out of the musical phrase, or other vital rhythms.

* In fact, many a dancer is seen to linger on the beat, toy with it, or peremptorily toss it aside. This procedure may not be recommended to novices, but it can become, if sparingly practiced, a charming quality with past-masters of the art.

To know musical rhythm well is indispensable to any dancer who uses music; and there are as yet few who dance without music.* Unfortunately, far too many dancers neglect that side of their education, and even call themselves interpretative dancers, without knowing much or anything about this basis of their interpretations. It would be much better for such dancers to begin to work without music. That would be at least an honest course to take.

The knowledge of rhythm, however, does not end with music. Rhythm comes to the dancer through manifold experience, a growth in sensibility and understanding. There is a physical, an emotional, a dynamic rhythm. (This latter has its correspondence in linear rhythm. See Appendix.) The first two are individual with each person; to know them, you must know yourself. Little can be taught about them; they are largely a matter of self-education and self-study. Together and, where music is being used, in conjunction with musical rhythm, they determine the fourth, and most evident—dynamic rhythm.

* See Glossary: Unaccompanied Dance.

PHYSICAL RHYTHM The clearest, although not the only, expression of physical rhythm is our way of breathing. How many people know much of their way of breathing, how many know anything about breathing at all, except a few professional singers, orators, speakers? Whilst our knowledge of breathing is very scant, it is a most important factor for the dancer to study.

By breathing we take part in the outside world, even though not speaking, not even thinking of it. It is the most ethereal, and admittedly, the most important function of our physical life. Common language has treated it as a synonym for life. We read of the "breath of life," and when a person stops breathing, people say, "all life has left him,"—an expression which is never used if a person merely stops looking, moving, or speaking. A stream of breath ascends, a stream descends: hope, joy, fear, well-being, ill-feeling, may play upon this stream in a thousand ways, the human will may retard it or hasten it, but it may never stop altogether as long as life lasts. It is life's pulse, life's rhythm.

The dancer will take good care of the opportunity to regulate this stream so that it may not give out and leave him wanting, or to check its impetuously throbbing power so that it may not overthrow the structure of motions which he is building up. Like any stream, breathing can be regulated. Sometimes, it is too powerful—if so, it easily threatens the slight fabric of balance, especially during slow transitions, and when a delicate motion is being carried to a stop or a climax. Then the dancer would have to know how to hold in, to check the outflow of this stream of breath momentarily, and be able to sustain an absolute pause.—Sometimes, breathing is too slack. Then rhythmic breathing exercises must work to lengthen the duration of inhalation, exhalation, *as well as the pause between*,* until a lasting gain in depth is achieved. On the whole, breathing must carry, support and sustain the dancer's action, subordinate itself to the rise and fall of motion in such a way that it appears as an individual primary or secondary rhythm within the musical or the action-rhythm. In certain cases, the new dancer will treat breathing as a visible

---

* This pause between inhalation and exhalation has rightly been called the "creative pause" from which a new impetus springs.

element of his dance. To enhance some expression, the physical action of breathing may become marked beyond its natural degree. The dancer can choose whether to make it of primary or of secondary importance, or rather, this choice is determined by the type of dancing that is being followed. The physical rhythm has only recently come to the fore in discussion of dancing matters; so far, most dancers have given it secondary importance. There are, however, some schools of which it is the leading principle. Some German schools are based on a special science of breathing. Of course, breathing is not the only evidence of man's physical rhythm but for the purpose of elucidating commonly valid aims and conceptions, it suffices to speak of the breathing rhythm, the main evidence of physical rhythm. The rest belongs to biological research, simple conjecture, and to the preoccupations of a few isolated systems of dancing.

Taken outside of its physical import, breathing is the symbol of dancing. A *stream ascends, a stream descends*; from this prototype of motion sprang man's first dance, and with it, his gratitude to the giver of life-force flowed onward and upward. Nothing more beautiful than the slow lifting of arms, nay of the whole being, with the ascending breath: the attitude of humility, of humble asking is the same. The neck, in slender curve, carries out the last end of the rising motion, the head tilts back, the half-open lips seem ready to speak: the gesture of the "adorant" marks the pause, a "creative pause" indeed in the fullest sense of the word. Refreshed, the whole body slowly withdraws into itself, the arms sink, rest, palms outward, carrying out the line of gratitude which finishes the spiritual cycle of breathing.

If a dancer should carry out the foregoing exercise in the way described he has followed the rule of *passive action*. The will remains passive, the impetus comes from the rhythm of individual feeling. The dancer has given up any scheme of predetermined movement; relaxing completely, and emptying both body and mind of all elements of resistance, he has yielded himself altogether to the rising and falling of the stream within. Here, the physical rhythm of breathing and the emotional rhythm of feeling happen to run parallel, but aside from not violating the physical rhythm in any way, *the rhythm of feeling has a life of its own*, and can act from independent motivations. In that case, the physical rhythm will *follow* the rhythm of feeling; at other times, the inverse is the case. The two are closely interwoven with each other, and the dancer answers each call as it comes. The difference between him and the ordinary person consists in a heightened sensibility.

This inner urge of breathing, for instance, small as it was, would not have produced any noticeable

[28]

action for the layman; a slight raising of the chest perhaps, that is all. To the dancer, trained to listen carefully to the most imperceptible changes within both his body and mind, it meant a call to action which he answered immediately. With him, the slight, invisible motion (emotion) of the mind can become translated into physical movement as easily as the mightier waves of passion which may sweep the ordinary person into action. Between the two, there is only a difference of degree. A dancer might well be called a person with whom the degree of mental and physical sensibility is such that he can express instantly in visible motion the smallest oscillations of his inner life. In dance improvisations, for instance, these gestures and motions are not preconceived but remain as latent potentialities at the bottom of dormant mind. They come to life, much as waterplants on the surface of a still lake will respond to the slightest commotion of winds and waves—to movements from the surface, or from the depth below.

Whether the cause promoting those vibrations within the dancer be physical or mental, they will find alike their echo in his dance. His task is not to analyze and to probe, but to give way to the stream of life, to express it, translate, and interpret it. If he is wise, he will use emotional rhythm with great discretion; his dignity must show him where to check it, his sense of balance of artistic proportions must bridle it, or it will burst the slender vessel of form without which art becomes chaos. Nothing is so absurd as gushing sentimentality exhibited for inspection; again, nothing is so far removed from the dance, this most living of all arts, than cold intellectualism.

Thus understood, the emotional rhythm will not be confused with emotionalizing, to use a dreadful word. I mean with it simply the sentiment and feeling which prompts the dance; without it, the dance would lack personality, character, warmth—whatever one might call that particular attribute which is indistinguishable from the artist's individuality. Every great dancer has a clearly marked emotional rhythm; every bad dancer has either too little or too much of it.

To have discovered this necessity for *impression preceding expression*—is one of the most important contributions of the Free Dance. Its motivation is largely from within. It shuns empty motions as one shuns empty words. A lot of motions, strung together and picked beforehand with the best intent of producing æsthetic appearances, may strike us as intolerable, if they have not been presented sincerely—that is, springing from a strong physical or mental necessity. That will immediately lend color and meaning, where meaningless babble would ensue without it.

Much intelligence is necessary in order to see this, yet intelligence alone will not suffice to fill this second, absolute demand of the Free Dance: sincerity. A cold, calculating mind may be the worst foe of this mode of dancing, where the student cannot get very far without knowing how to yield. How to yield himself simply and trustingly, like a child, to the lead of the different rhythms playing in him, around him, be it music, the song of his own soul, the dynamic action-mood of his body which bid him to answer by dancing. However, the dancer may not despise intelligence; he will need it just where he most desperately strives for expression. He will need to train his body so that it can follow instantly the dictates from within or without, be quickly responsive to changes of rhythm and of meter. The mentally dull, the physical sluggard too, will invariably remain behind in the race, before even these elementary stages are mastered. There is constant interplay between intelligence and feeling in the necessities confronting the dancer, and it would be futile to try and dissociate one from another. Listening to the various currents of rhythm is not enough: he must possess a high degree of quick coördination and adaptability in order to be able to follow, and deep original feeling and skill, in order to translate them acceptably. Besides, he must develop group-feeling in ensemble work, perhaps the most difficult work of all. Ensemble work is again a question of sensibilities—of quick adjustment. It needs a keen sense of perception of the ever fluctuating state of the group mind as well as of the action; it also requires a high degree of individual initiative (by which each member may become the leader of all), checked by a voluntary self-denial in the quest of the larger common aim. This is only made possible by a deep feeling of love and sympathy with the work in hand. Again, the emotional and intellectual strata commingle one becomes the prerequisite of the other.

Music will do much to
heighten the sensibility of
the pupil, and certain sys-
tems try to achieve the training in sensibility by
a carefully worked out parallelism between musical rhythm and motor-action of the body. The
training in accuracy of keeping time, following
the intricacies of the musical phrase, and becoming alive to the detail as well as the unity of a
piece of music, of a whole composition: these are three
steps, gradually increasing in difficulty, which should
not be missing in the training of any dancer who
uses music. It may be counted as one of the greatest
achievements of the Dalcroze system to have shown
the Free Dance the importance of this. However, in
practice these three stages make their foremost appeal
to qualities of the mental, not of the emotional realm.
They promote ready coördination, concentrated attention, quick thought and adaptability, they *regulate*
by means of the musical, the physical rhythm, they
also doubtless call for some feeling where interpretation necessitates an intuitive response to music; but

[33]

on the whole, they treat the physical, emotional and dynamic rhythms as secondary matter. The pupil becomes an instrument of registering music *—the outcome of somebody else's thoughts and emotions, —and he is constantly concentrating upon modes of feeling and thinking which originated outside of himself.

If we compare this with the definition of the Dance as given on page 21 it does not appear that the dancer's task can be limited even by the widest scope given to his musical training. He must be aware of the fact that his art possesses much likeness to music, without as yet being identical with the latter. He will fail to realize a wealth of beauty if he does not cultivate that likeness, but he will prostitute his art, on the other hand, if he neglects to develop its uniqueness, the qualities inherent in the dance alone. The dancer is not only the instrument, but creator and performer as well.

The human body is like an organ with a thousand registers, all different in tone; but the main registers of the Dance lie along the lines where the dynamic

* This feeling of being an instrument of registering the measurable values in music, as the beat, etc., easily leads to a mechanization of the body.

rhythm and the rhythm of feeling predominate. "Musical parallelism" brings out some interesting possibilities for the Dance, but it is, at its best, an intellectual puzzle. The true analogies of music and dance lie in a direction where they are seldom sought: the musicality of the Dance—if I be permitted such an expression—is embodied for the Dance in its own preëminent means of expression, the dynamics of motion. This brings us to the fourth, most important factor of rhythmic realization: the dynamic rhythm.

DYNAMIC RHYTHM *The arc of inner tension* that connects the beginning with the end of a motion, *may be called dynamic rhythm.*

In this form, the definition recalls music—the sign which symbolizes the phrase in musical notation: ⌒ The phrase mark means for the musician: play this connectedly, hold it together as an idea separate from the next. In like manner, the dancer's task is to know how to mark clearly *the beginning, the path, the end* of a motion.* What musicianship means in a musician, the dynamic sense means to the dancer.

It expresses itself in the way he literally *carries* his motion, like something precious in every detail which is entrusted to his care. He deftly starts on the motion,** designs its path boldly or quietly, as it may

---

* Compare the careless placing of feet with beginners—as if the touch of the foot on the floor were not a moment of greatest importance to the dancer!

** Whilst such "clean work" is necessary to the training of a dancer, just as smooth fingering is to the musician, later the dancer will learn how to efface, or bridge the gap between one movement and another. These transitions must not become forced; only too often they become moments of embarrassment to the dancer who then resorts to some quickly substituted sundry action, called "padding." Transitions should not be "padded" but ought to lead most naturally and smoothly over into the next movement.

[36]

be, but always enjoying it or sending his feeling along every second of its way; eagerly pushing up to its climax, if it is energized action, or marking the sensation of floating, of being drawn by the emotional rhythm, if it is passive action. A thrilling moment of perfect equilibrium, often an actual moment of floating, of being suspended in mid-air, separates the ascending from the descending path of motion.

Here the dynamic impetus emanating from the starting point is spent, motion has come to a standstill whilst feeling or emotion has come to a climax; sometimes the force of the motion itself has been stored up into a last tremendous effort, when the arc of tension neared its crest: in either case, the dancer possessing dynamic feeling will do his utmost to give this moment of suspension inner weight, dwelling on it as long as he can, enjoying his victory over space, time, or gravity, as the case might be. Inexperienced dancers are apt to toss this important moment aside, although their sense of self-preservation should point to the opposite. These moments of suspension (in energized action) are often the only moments of respite the dancer has during his work; a wise person will make the most of it * and thus save, at the same time, an important element of expression. The impression of elegance or ease permeating a dance results, for the greatest part, from a skillful handling of the *crest of motion*. The dancer must know how to project his feeling of a creative pause upon the spectator in order to give the impression of mastery in unlabored motion. It helps the imagination to conceive of air in such moments as something which can actually carry; then the dancer will ride, so to speak, on the crest of his action, as if weight were cast aside.

The next moment, though, gravity will carry him down. The *descending path* of the motion is of no lesser importance than the ascending. Now the dancer will measure how much weight to give to it. If lightness should be expressed, he will hold in on the stream of force, let go gradually and so give the impression of an effortless gliding down. (An impression, however, which should amount to actual experience with the dancer.) In expression dancing, on the contrary, the element of heaviness is often stressed beyond the measure of physical necessity

* These moments will usually coincide with the pause between inhalation and exhalation.

in order to add weight to some dramatic action.

At any rate, the descending path of the motion is in the Free Dance not given over to optic deceptions, as frequently in the ballet, where much effort is being spent on making every downward motion appear feather-weight. Weightless action, where weight would speak most loudly!

Music recognizes no difference in importance between up-beat and down-beat, but quantitatively, the heavy beat bears the accent. In like manner, the New Dance conceives of up-stroke and down-stroke as paramount elements lending their lightness or their weight to the construction of the dance. The tendency is to emphasize elements of construction as such, rather than to conceal them.*

Besides up-stroke and down-stroke, and the crest of

* A tendency, which links up the Free Dance with modern architecture, such as we know it since the beginning of the twentieth century. That both should have found simultaneously the same dynamic principle, is certainly significant, and should help to destroy the popular theory—that the Free Dance is but a creation of a passing wave of fashion and an outcome of weakly fancy. The *building* of the Free Dance rests on a sound basis, although its style may as yet appear somewhat undefined. This, time can and will remedy. A quarter of a century is little for an art to crystallize. At any rate, we have at last a form of dancing which bears the stamp of the time in which we live; which is, for the better or for the worse, a living art for us.

the arc of movement between them, *the end of the motion* receives equal attention from the dancer. The end of the arc of tension may be the complete dying out of a motion, like notes of music, which, left to linger to the last, finally vanish into space. Such a complete rest occurs seldom in the midst of a dance, but it is frequent as illustration of the last notes of music in a musical interpretation. (Inexperienced dancers, and especially all beginners, are apt to "drop" this end, instead of holding it.) This hold on the last end of passive motion, whether ascending or descending, is rather different from the energized hold in motion-climax. Again, the end of the descending path (imagined in continuous motion) may be like a motion-climax: a brief creative pause each time, filling itself with vigor and feeling for the new ascent. In this case, the down-stroke had not spent its energies altogether, but descending quickly, has only sought the brief touchdown for a strong new bouncing up. (Compare the skip.) Thus we get from the motion a deciding feeling of up-rhythm. The prevailing rhythm is always the one which is particularly stressed by the dancer, and this effect may be achieved irrespective of time-values. A good skip should give the impression of up-rhythm; the stronger the bouncing up, or up-stroke, the longer, however, will be the downward path. Here, up-rhythm and length of time are in an inverse relation to each other. Downward rhythm may be equally marked by stress as for instance, in stamping; as a rule, though, the *accent* in the downward path is obtained by lengthening it, at the same time applying relaxed motion. In this case, the end of the motion is already apprehended by the descending motion, which lingers on towards the end without losing its impetus altogether, so that an ever renewed small rising is contrasted by a slow falling, long lingering, imperceptible end. (Passive action.)

THE DANCE, AND
MUSIC

The dynamic rhythm in dancing has a great deal in common with the rhythm of music. In each case, every moment is the cradle for the next, one already contained in the other by unfailing laws. This *apprehending* of the next moment (movement), as well as the full realization of the rhythm of the moment; the entering into the swing of the current of movement with the whole being—characterize both the execution of music and of dancing. They work with the same values: stress (accent), tempo, up- and downward rhythm, high-low connotations,* and the inter-relation of these values is the same in most cases. Dancing knows consonance and dissonance, and the two elements of melody and harmony. The former is carried out in linear progression of space patterns.** The latter, too, is beginning to appear in compositions en

* The Dance carries out much of the musical notation: crescendo, decrescendo, forte, piano, legato, staccato, rallentando—all can find their application. The Dance is an eminently musical art. (This expression almost seems a misstatement in the face of the fact that the beginnings of music have arisen with, or out of the Dance.) But it is at the same time evident that a dancer could express all the foregoing values also without musical accompaniment.

** Compare Chapter 2 of *Building Stones*, and Appendix (Space Patterns).

[42]

masse which make a contrapuntal treatment possible; there, the melodic line is traced as against a background of bigger choral movement.

These are the values which both the Dance and music derive from an inheritance out of a common start, in the past: and the dancer shares with the musician the knowledge and use of some laws inherent in time-progression.

Such sharing constitutes an advantage, if well done, but a great danger, if poorly understood. The dancer and music must remain the worst enemies, unless they choose to become the best friends. The development of the last two centuries shows that a harmonious adjustment is perfectly possible. It must not be forgotten, that from Gluck to Haydn, there existed a close coöperation between the dance and music; that even the glorious discovery of the symphonic form leads back to the times where the composer received direct inspiration from dance forms which were then the common property of the people, and the Dance, in turn, was imperceptibly modified by changes introduced in the time, and the character, of music. Later, music outdistanced the Dance by leaps and bounds, taking full possession of the unlimited possibilities of a polyphonic development which finally gave us this greatest gift of modern western art, the symphony; whilst the Dance, engrossed in laying down the laws for a perennial art-form, lost by and by all contact with the surrounding realities, remained definitely behind, and became a divertissement and adjunct to the opera, where it would still be, unless the enterprising twentieth century—and incidentally, Isadora Duncan—had rescued it from sure oblivion, or death.

Since then, much has happened. The tendency of the moment points in the direction of enmity between the Dance and music. This development,—however strongly entrenched in some parts of the globe,—is as yet too recent here to have gone beyond the stage of conjecture for us.

Part II

COMPARISONS

COMPARISON BETWEEN THE BALLET AND THE
RHYTHMIC DANCE

Between a bewildered public and a groping host of students on the one hand, and the few initiated dancers on the other, there seems to be at present an impassable gulf, called typological differences. This gulf, like an uncharted sea, is dotted with innumerable islands, each representing a different type in the Dance. If one could but take a foothold on the nearest of those islands, from there go on to the next, and so on farther and farther through the gulf, it could possibly be forded and conquered. Fascinating it would be—but who has the time to visit those thousand islands, the wisdom to start right on the road, the courage to meet its obstacles, the patience to go through with such an exhaustive search?

The difficulties are not so overwhelming if we look first to some point from which a broad view of the whole may be obtained. If I should have to compare and to classify these many different islands where the Dance has anchored its hopes, I should attempt to do so from the two islands that loom much larger than all the rest, that is, the vantage points of the Ballet and the Free Dance. Then it would soon become clear that these islands, confusing though their number may seem, are not so many isolated units, but they belong, archipelago fashion, to two or three main systems. Among those main systems the Ballet and the Free Dance stand out for their obvious difference in structural quality, the one representing the "Rock of Ages," tradition, the other the new attitude of the twentieth century, which not only accepts the present but keeps an expectant eye turned toward the future.

Comparisons along general lines are not very informing. If we would gain a real basis for the understanding of typological distinctions in the Dance we must first of all examine when and why it came to the breaking point where an old system was all of a sudden confronted by a host of new attempts at a different type of dancing.

It was undoubtedly Isadora Duncan who caused this revolution in the Dance at the beginning of this century, after the ballet had held sway undisturbed and unchallenged for three hundred years—three hundred years of a steady evolution along the lines of the same principle that had guided its start. It is not my purpose to make here an exhaustive survey of the art of Isadora Duncan, as this study is given over to general principles underlying the barefoot dance. However, such a study could not proceed without stating the fact which some dance enthusiasts are now too prone to overlook: that the beginning of the New Dance *was* Isadora Duncan. Any near-correct appraisal of Isadora's contribution to the art of the Dance would have to deal at length with the background whose dusty cobwebs she lifted one by one; and it would have to measure the immeasurable—the irradiations of an extraordinarily powerful and magnetic personality. To the theme of her glowing personality most of the literature up to date has been dedicated. It is most difficult to free oneself even for a moment from this overwhelming impression and yet, for the sake of arriving at the entirely impersonal fact of her immediate technical contribution to the Dance, we must be ready to do so.

Isadora brought us the free rhythmic attack on motion. She was probably quite unaware of it herself. To her, technical details were of secondary importance, as she was primarily concerned with a portrayal of emotional significance. But the incidental result was nevertheless the technique of a new attack on motion, and the dance-world became electrified by the discovery of a freely flowing line, evolving "other movements in unending sequence of still higher and greater expression," in other words, the secret of rhythmic rebirth. Isadora has been repeatedly charged with not having any technique at all. Hers was a technique so veiled in emotional values and so immediately the outgrowth of her own artistic purpose that it was not a technique *to be taught*. It could only be guessed at, and few could do that. A few, though, clearly perceived the significance of an ultra-individual technique and built upon it by induction a method which has come to be known as the rhythmic method.

It is this method which I make the basis of the comparison with the Ballet, since a concrete type had to be chosen. Rhythmic dancing is not considered here as a fixed form but as a method. Whatever one may think of the value of the Rhythmic Dance as a form, its method undoubtedly has served all the pioneers of the first two decades of the twentieth century. The rhythmic attack on motion holds sway even in the

Dance of most "modernistic" tendencies to-day, just as it had caused the breaking away from the Ballet for countless followers of the neo-Grecian* idea, much earlier in the century. Only the emphasis is different: the latter stressed the musical and emotional rhythm, whereas the new German Dance and kindred varieties seek their inspiration mainly in the dynamic rhythm. Each focuses its work from a different angle within the same structure; and that structure is built by the four rhythmic dimensions with which the Free Dance is, in my opinion, concerned.

This different angle, though, produced a result so much unlike the former that it became immediately apparent a new phase of the Free Dance would have to be counted from the appearance of the new German mode. If I hold nevertheless in my comparison to the Rhythmic Dance as typically representing the Free Dance, it is not from a predilection for the Rhythmic Dance nor from a prejudice against the (more modern) German Dance with which I have been acquainted for ten years. This latter type— which bears at present here the awkward name of "modernistic" dancing—has only just begun to make

* See Glossary.

itself felt in a few large cities of the East, and is as yet far from making an appreciable impression on America as a whole. I prefer, therefore, to take the more commonly known Rhythmic Dance as the starting point for my comparison. It not only represents the starting point of the Free Dance as far as the chronological order is concerned, but it also represents the working basis for numberless subdivisions of the Free Dance such as practiced to-day by the great majority of barefoot schools, a few outstanding schools of the "modernistic" type notwithstanding. Even that type has been grafted recently on a basis of the rhythmic order.

I mean to compare here the rank and the file of the barefoot schools with the rank and the file of the ballet schools. This fact must not be lost sight of in reading the Comparison between the Ballet and the Rhythmic Dance. The Ballet has produced Pavlova and Nijinsky, but such as they belong to an order of genius which always succeeds independently—and sometimes in spite—of any form. Although we are glad to think of the splendid achievements of the great artists among the ballet masters, the characterization which appears in the following pages holds true of ninety-nine out of a hundred commercial ballet schools. It is likewise true that the Free Dance has much to learn from the Ballet. The importance of a comparison does not lie in establishing one greater than the other but in showing the possibilities of entirely different approaches to the Dance: the traditional and the individual—not to say: inspirational—approach.

The Ballet   and   The Rhythmic Dance

The æsthetic creed here is a belief in a code of absolutely valid rules. Many of them spring from the æsthetic conceptions of the court of Louis XIV, Louis XV, Louis XVI, and still enter largely into the Ballet of to-day.

The Rhythmic Dance holds all values to be relative, dependent one upon another. Accordingly, æsthetics is the sum total from varying sources, and combines the artistic feeling of the present time with the best æsthetic knowledge of past epochs.

If the Ballet were to define its idea of beauty, geometric laws would hold the preponderance in such a definition. These geometric laws are in turn modified by the accumulated sum of æsthetic laws which date several centuries back. From this strict code of laws one, however, is barred by common consent: the law of gravity must not find expression.

The Rhythmic Dance makes one law ruling in its understanding of what should be beautiful: sincerity of expression is the foremost demand. Outside of that, the dancer may formulate his æsthetic laws for himself, as any other artist does. His own potentialities and critical perception are his guides.

* The Comparison is so arranged that each paragraph under the heading "Ballet" has a corresponding paragraph in the opposite column, under the heading "Rhythmic Dance."

[54]

The ideal type of the Ballet strikes the modern taste as feminine. There is so little essential difference between the type of male and female dancers in the Ballet because it originated in a period when the attire for men and women was rather alike, and corseted waists imposed the same type of limited movement upon both the feminine and masculine body.

The underlying logic is one of mechanics.

The individual, physical rhythm is suppressed.

The linear rhythm is the main source of inspiration. The dynamic rhythm is strictly measured, subject to the rhythm of line.

With reference to musical rhythm, the attention is centered on the most mechanical coincidence of all the time-values common to both music and the Dance: the *beat*.

Much of the male type enters into the athletic aspect of many dances. In early Grecian times, dancers were warriors; women entered the ranks only later. Some of this genealogy is reflected even in these late offshoots from an originally rather athletic conception of the Dance. (See Rhythmic Dance in Glossary.)

The logical system rests on rhythm.

The physical rhythm is made visibly manifest.

The dynamic rhythm is the main source of inspiration; it is guided by the rhythm of line, and by the musical rhythm, where music is used. When not, the dynamic rhythm is preëminent.

The metric subdivisions of the beat are followed where their importance within the larger aim of the musical phrase demands it. As a rule, the *phrase* is treated by

[55]

This assures great precision in quick motions, but it also breaks up the dynamic rhythm into many small units which detract from the main stream of motion, and of music as well. Thus, the favorite time of ballet dancing has become a very quick, staccato musical rhythm.

The emotional rhythm is concealed in favor of a stationary expression of ease.

On the whole, it may be said that the ballet conquers rhythm by putting other values, mostly of a decorative, or kinetic-mechanistic character, into the foreground of consideration.

The paramount aim is to create an impression of *lightness*. Therefore the main attention of the Ballet is centered on an outwitting of gravity.

the Rhythmic Dance as the unit of first importance. The Rhythmic Dance, with its ideal of long lines along curves, naturally seeks the larger musical subdivisions, with their longer ascending and descending arch. It probably finds its best opportunity in legato time.

Whether the tempo be quick or slow, the emotional rhythm finds its expression.

Thus, the aim is to bring out rhythm in its four-fold character; in fact, some exponents of Rhythmic Dancing have made rhythm an end in itself to the point where it may have defeated their *dance*.

Lightness and weight are treated as equal factors, each capable of imparting interest to the Dance. The Rhythmic Dance has *restored weight* to its place as an important element in the organization of a Dance composition, just as it is an important factor in the space distribution of painting and of sculpture.

This ideal directs the attack on motion. The Ballet needs quick lifting and sinking action; circling, to help the body gyrate and to lift itself on its axis, as if weightless. All this dictates motion from the *joints*, or articulations; the emphasis upon the airy aspect of spinning, twirling, leaping, necessitates the turning out of the foot in the ankle joint, and turning out of thigh in hip joint, —in other words, a sideways disposition of arms and legs. This is done in accordance with the tendency to present to the spectator a frontal view. Symmetry is much favored, and where the symmetric law is deviated from, there is a strict observance of certain counter-balance positions, the space pattern remaining the same for everybody, irrespective of the lines which the individual body presents. A uniform law re-

Studying lightness and weight in their alternating stages, the Rhythmic Dance directs most of its movement through *muscular control*, or pull-and-relaxation action, measuring all the time how much value to give to the elements of time and stress. Such motion proceeds from the farthest point of attack, along sustained lines. In quick action this is somewhat less marked. The Rhythmic Dance sees the basic evolution of man in the *forward* trend. Hence all walking, running, leaping are built on a straight foot-placing: the front-back motion of the hip is more developed than the sideways motion. The tendency is to face in the main direction of the motion. Thus we get an all-round view of the body without much concern as to its symmetric arrangement. The disposition of the arms, too,

[57]

garding æsthetics and balance is imposed: the method is dogmatic.

It implies that the Ballet has found the sum total of kinæsthetic possibilities, which can be exactly described and cataloged. Thus the Ballet appears in two parallel strains: the artistic aspect has a scientific counterpart. (There is some contradiction in the fact, though, that the findings are held as final and universally satisfactory. If anything, science and art have this much in common: their findings are hardly ever final; they are forever in flux, prey to the processes of an endless evolution.)

The Ballet, however, seems to have more trust in its science (the law), than in its art (individual creative expression), because it seeks the fulfillment of its aims by admitting more obedience (a form of will) than thought in its mode of work, and by sub-

follows not so much in opposition, as in accord with the main direction of the movement.—This method largely relies on the individual to find his own laws of balance, and to seek lines and modes of expression satisfactory to him. It is, in this respect, experimental, empiric. It holds the realm of kinæsthetic exploration to be as endless as the changing lessons of human taste, and as the varying aspects of individual human longings, which must forever try to *harmonize the present, immediate experiences* of life by pouring them into the vaster mold of art forms.

In the process of artistic creation, form is filled with spirit, when the will achieves oneness with thought and feeling, and they unite in a concrete expression. The aims of the Rhythmic Dance are in accord with this definition.

[58]

stituting knowledge for feeling.

This knowledge is, as it
were, the professional secret
of the artist; the spectator
gets little or no chance to
share it.

The motion is produced as
a finished result from causes
which seem hidden; the construction is veiled, inasmuch
as it happens most of the time
too quickly for the eye to
follow—as if produced by a
charm. The numerous stops
and new starts in action, connecting—or dividing—otherwise unconnected small motions, add to this impression.
This impression is a by-
product of the method of
assembling the action by
stringing together separate
units of motion, called
"steps." The dividing lines
are the "Attitudes" and "Positions." Each motion, or
step, should begin and end
in one of the Five Positions.
The stationary element, or

The construction of the
motion is exposed; it *grows*
before the eyes of the spectator, who is thus allowed to
participate with his own
kinæsthetic feeling.

Speed is not a foremost
consideration. Although the
rhythmic Dance achieves
great speed in the leg motions—in running, leaping,
skipping, sliding,—it favors
a slower but continuous flow
of motion.

However, the Rhythmic
Dance recognizes the value
of the pause, not as a stop
and interruption, but as a
halt and a moment of recreation in consecutive action.
Rhythmic dancing takes its
cue largely from organic
growth. Organic growth
knows no fixed formula;
and even thought happens,
pauses, then takes a new
flight. The pictures in the
Rhythmic Dance arise from
the thought-content, and are

the position, is thus given the place of first importance—all in keeping with the emphasis upon the decorative side, and linear rhythm.

In the "steps" and "attitudes" consists the alphabet of the Ballet. They remain always the same, are minutely cataloged, and the grammar consists of clever rearrangements of the separate units, that are treated somewhat in the form of a picture puzzle—gathered by a process of *accretion*.

Thus, the Ballet shows a greater variety and frequency of changes, smaller subdivisions in action, quick transitions which go more or less through the same paths (five positions).

The aspect of cleverness, to which we already referred,

transmuted in motion—a process of inspiration which might be rather called *unfolding* than applying preconceived notions.

There are few fixed motions, but the dancer should command a great variety of inflections, and be capable of *evolving*, in line with the general principle, motions to suit the thought-content of his own dance compositions.

As the Rhythmic Dance avoids abrupt dividing lines in the interest of sequential movement, transitions are, or seem, slower; each movement follows from the preceding one through the logic of rhythmic rebirth.*

This prompts, in the last analysis, the impression of

* Compare the ideal of Isadora Duncan: "The primary or fundamental movements of the new school of the Dance must have within them the seed from which will evolve all other movements, each in turn to give birth to others in unending sequence of still higher and greater expressions."

[60]

is a result of this. The Ballet dazzles the spectator through prowess of motions whose artifice seems incomprehensible.

The motion thus appears as an end in itself, and it is presented with a delight in effusion, and much elaboration of detail. The ideal is *variety*: it naturally relegates expression to the second place, since the intricate mechanics of movement require the paramount attention of the dancer.

The ballet dancer never seems to forget his effect upon the spectator: when he dances, he exhibits a lesson extremely well learned.*

The moods of the Ballet tend to gayety, preciosity, and in the heavier type, to a certain pompousness.

"naturalness" which the spectator gets. The rhythmic dancer presents in artistic form, a common rhythmic experience, the universally accessible.

Motion is here the means to an end of expression, and it is used with economy—a ruling factor in most of the artistic production of our times. This voluntary restriction as to diversity of motion secures, instead, *an intensity of expression.*

The rhythmic dancer presents a seemingly spontaneous experience, which the spectator shares.

The Rhythmic Dance lends itself especially well to simplicity, restraint, heroism; while nobility, grandeur, tenderness, struggle, doubt, joy are some of the favorite moods.

* In this respect, the Free Dance has yet to learn from the example of the Ballet.

Thus the Ballet appears as a form of spectacular dancing, exhibiting great accomplishment for admiration. The ballet dancer is the supreme showman and entertainer, and thus serves a widespread need.*

Humbleness is not in his make-up, nor can it be. He always appears as the victor —a victor over restrictive laws. His action seems to flee the ground, his is the pretense at independence from the ground; and he lives happily unaware of his enslavement to the inexorable laws of convention.

Probably by sheer law of contrast, it has turned its attention away from the showy side of the Dance, and reverted somewhat to the original form, the Dance of devotional or sacrificial character, sometimes playing into the realm of nature forces. The rhythmic dancer recognizes his indebtedness to the ground: but his action grows away from it. He humbly acknowledges his origin, whilst he reaches up to the realms of a superior guiding force.** The Dance has become for him once more the projection of an inner state of mind. Recognizing that, he practices it consciously or unconsciously as an art.

* Showmanship may be an art. It is not the aim of this book, however, to decide what place the Ballet occupies in the art of to-day. The reader who is anxious to follow up this issue will find an excellent summary of the position of the Ballet with respect to the artistic feeling and standards of to-day, in Cecil Sharp's book, *The Dance.*

** The most modern Dance has just entered an entirely new phase, and is approaching the field of psychology and sociology for interesting subject-matter.

The most evident difference between the Rhythmic Dance and the Ballet probably lies in the center of movement from which each draws the impetus for its motions.

The Ballet sees its strongest support in a straight and rather rigid spinal column.* Whatever action is taken, radiates from this vertical, which rests on the pelvic belt. Here lies the strongest point of attack for the Ballet; with its emphasis on leg motion, this lower pole becomes in the Ballet the more articulate center of motion, whilst the waist line marks the sharp division between this, and the less used upper one.** Through this division in a lower and an upper story the body feels cut in two, and often looks it. It lacks unity. The motion is scattered, and easily produces

* An inheritance from the tightly laced bodice of the sixteenth century.
** The arms utilize only a limited field of the spatial possibilities open to them, on account of a rigidly enforced system of geometric planes, which may intersect, but at one point only; the relation of these planes to each other remains expressed through an angle of ninety degrees. There are a thousand possibilities besides these two requirements. They are, however, disregarded in favor of the precision which this system of self-imposed limitations ensures.

[63]

an impression of restlessness. Possessing all the virtue of its defects, this system is one that makes for the utmost efficiency of motion, and that efficiency in turn has contributed its share to the aspect of restlessness. Each member is assigned to a certain function, like so many wheels in a machine. Touch one of these wheels, and it reels off the desired motion with utter promptness. The body is an instrument of efficiency: This fact we are seldom allowed to forget in the Ballet. All the time we see, as it were, the skeleton of its machinery.

How could it be otherwise, since the Ballet works from the skeleton. It moves from the *joints,* and evolves its kinetic action in lever fashion and in circling fashion, from two poles at the opposite ends of the spine; favoring, as we stated already, symmetry, a full frontal view with much widening of the linear possibilities in the vertical plane,* sideways to the right and left of the spine (see diagram on opposite page, p. 65).

The extremities seem to be radiating from the trunk, loosely attached. They are sharply articulated. The first analogy that comes to the mind in view of these

* See Appendix, Chapter on Planes.

diagrams is the insect body. Such likeness may rest on a deep inner bond between the two: the insect must fly, and the ballet dancer would like to.

SYNTHETIC IMPRESSION OF BALLET ACTION

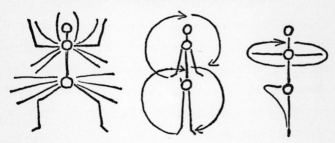

The Rhythmic Dance, as an offshoot of the neo-Grecian dance revival, knows but one center of force.*

In adopting the upper center of movement, the Rhythmic Dance automatically expanded the arm motion and restricted the leg action. But aside from these effects, the choice of this center is of the utmost importance for the general quality of the dance. By some laws which are hardly traceable in their inter-

* About Isadora's seeking "the central spring of all movement, the crater of motor power, the unity from which all divisions of movements are born," we have the following reference: "For hours I would stand quite still, my two hands folded between my breasts. . . . After many months, when I had learned to concentrate all force to this Center I found that hereafter when I listened to music the rays and vibrations of the music streamed to this one fount of light within me. . . ."

relation of ethical and æsthetic import, it has restored much dignity to the dance. The higher aspirations of the race seem to have worked from this upper center; maybe they have developed it.

In the evolution of the body, the line of progress points upward. Animals use four extremities to support themselves. Man needs but two. Our physical advantage over the animal lies in the erect spine which frees the anterior extremities for purposes that have nothing to do with the carrying and propelling of the bodily weight. In the measure as the impression of weight can be taken off from even the lower extremities, the upward-soaring tendency of the body becomes emphasized.

Whatever tension there was, the Greeks, for instance, sought to gather into this upper center of energy, the point under the chest where organs of vital significance lie hidden. The protective armor of the ribs shelters the main source of physical rhythm, the heart-beat and the respiration. At the same time, here is a flexible armor, capable of contraction and expansion. Thus this center becomes expressive of the undulating motion of rising and falling; the converging of the ribs to one point in front serves furthermore that significant folding-un-folding process of which we shall speak later.

If we may draw general conclusions from a study of Greek statuary, it is apparent that certain tangible æsthetic results follow from the development of this upper center of energy for kinetic uses. Flowing from one starting point, the lines of the body become lengthened, at least for the lower part. This results in a natural looking arrangement of gentle curves,* which gave the Greek body an aspect of repose even in action. Such an impression is invariably conditioned by a complete mastery of muscular relaxation and tension. This mastery, the Greeks doubtless possessed. A potent factor in developing it may have been just this upper center of action: the economy of focusing both thought and action on one main point, drawing all the forces upward where lightness came to meet them. It rendered to the Greek form those inexpressibly noble lines that seemed to bespeak the dignity of man as reposing in the freedom of a consciously regulated power.

* This seemingly careless arrangement avoids right-angle positions, as well as the strict display of symmetry in the body. The idea that the Greeks exploited symmetry as an æsthetic or decorative factor in the body, is hardly borne out by the statuary of the best epoch.

Similarly, the lines in the Rhythmic Dance flow as much as possible, unbroken from this center of force and lightness. They have unconsciously followed the softer curves of young, growing things: stems and branches curving up, and out, softening the angle. Nature, at least in plant life, seems to avoid the sharp right angle. This form-organization is prevalent throughout the floral patterns of Greek decorative art, and of renaissance design. It lends to æsthetics an element of tenderness as well as of ordered restraint.

That restraining and calling back to oneness of action and tone was one of the main attainments of Rhythmic Dancing. If it had achieved the development and variation of form as well as this basic organization—if the imaginative element had caught up with the organizatory—it would stand to-day as the Dance supreme of America.

Every system, or organization, carries within itself the causes of its own limitations. As it was, the ideal of continuous progression or sequential motion led the followers of Grecian dance forms to exploit those natural forms of movement where each becomes the source of the next: as walking, running, skipping or bouncing. The same tendency required, in the line of spatial orientation, the one which offered the least resistance to continuous forward motion: the circle, that age-old formation of communal dancing. Once in a circle, you never need to stop. Straight lines, and sideways progressions necessitate a constant re-orientation, halt and return. Neither Isadora's early work, nor the Rhythmic Dance at its inception favored halts, and both worked in half-consciously imposed limitations, that were due, in the last analysis, to their choice of the upper center of force.

The motion, localized to this upper center, and seeking long lines along curves, rather than angles, had to result in the *swing* as the main action for speed, —where the ballet uses the kick—and the pull-relax (or unfolding-folding) motion as the main action for slow movement. Prompted, furthermore, by the ideal of *continuity* of unbroken motion, we have many profile positions, the *forward* moving orientation necessitating *straight* foot-placing (the beautiful swinging step is very characteristic of this form of the Dance) and leg motions mostly swinging straight back and forward from that upper center of force, whilst the circling motion of the hips remains largely unused.

This kinetic action suggests the following diagrams:

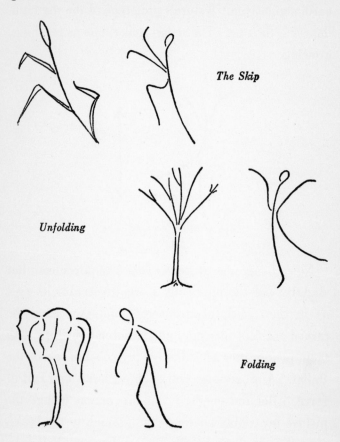

The Skip

Unfolding

Folding

ACTION-MODES OF THE FREE DANCE, AND THEIR
NATURAL PROTOTYPES

Thus we get the flowing lines, a flow down as well as up; the dancer appears as the mediator between earth and heaven. Nature's prototype of the rhythmic dancer is the tree. The action strikes one as reaching, growing.

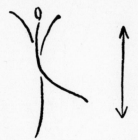

The vertical, "growing" line

Now change the aforementioned requirements but slightly; use the hips fully in their circular as well as in their back-forward sense, and you have the turned-out foot placing, and the turned-out hips with their possibilities of sideways progression, as in the Ballet. A progression full of stops, jerks, and full of force. But the emphasis on hip action brings the picture invariably nearer to the ground, to the heaviness of animalistic recollections. Thus the ballet defeats sometimes its own ends through much efficiency,

[71]

whilst endeavoring, on the other end of the line, to present as its favorite aspect, floating, flying; the horizontal miraculously suspended in space.

The horizontal, "floating" line

The attention is then directed away from the natural basis of the dancer as a human being; if he could be consistent, or sincere, he would be forgiven. However, he is supposed to be an apparition only, a mirage of himself, the elusive unattainable—a fata morgana. This appearance shares, like all apparitions, the fate of being too fleeting. The dancer has to come down to earth, a fact which is treated only as an accident. But these accidents happen too often, and the continuity of the action is constantly broken into. The ballet dancer flees from a despised into a favored element, from the earth into the air; the rhythmic dancer

[72]

embraces and understands both. The ballet dancer is foe of the one, master of the other; the rhythmic dancer is friend of both.

If the moods and methods of the Free Dance differ essentially from the Ballet, they are also different from Folk Dancing and National Dancing.

Most of the forms of the Ballet can be traced to some Folk or National Dance. From the village, where they originated, these forms were transplanted in the time of the early renaissance to the courts, and there adapted and reshaped by the ballet masters, according to prevailing needs and customs. Along this road from village-green to court, and thence to the opera-ballet, which these country-dances traveled,* many of their characteristics were thoroughly changed; their original vigor and liveliness usually gave way to a sedate stateliness, often stiffness, but steps originally very simple were as often elaborated upon and complicated by the ballet process. Whatever likeness there may be, though, remains, and is traceable in the so-called "steps"; and it is the "step" —a fixed form evolved or elaborated upon by con-

* See Cecil Sharp's excellent book, *The Dance: An Historical Survey of Dancing in Europe.*

[74]

vention,—which binds the seemingly so different forms of dancing together: the humble Folk Dance and the virtuoso Ballet.

Both were tied to this method by a common wish: that for entertainment, recreation.

They both arose out of the need for communal dancing. Their difference was only one of caste. In the time of the "masques," a band of dancers from the streets could enter and invite the king to dance with them. Later, the court summoned dancing masters to teach them some of the dances which the commoners enjoyed. The early corps de ballet were recruited from among the nobles themselves. Later, when the courts maintained their ballet schools, the more exacting parts of the ballet were carried by professionals, but the action was preceded, interspersed, or followed by the dances in which the entire court took part. Thus, the Ballet has its reason for being, both as an entertainment and as a form of communal recreation. It may seem somewhat unusual, to conceive of a court as a community, but at least in those times we speak of, the courts asserted their right to recreation just as any other, less pretentious, community would. From the effort to organize this community recreation sprung the Ballet, and so complete was the success, that recreation became labor, and had to be taken off the hands of the courts, who then began to hire their professional entertainers, and preferred to watch them from the opera boxes.

The aspect of recreation was of course more evident in the country-dances, where the villagers—and towns-folk alike—sought surcease from the heavier labors of the day. Any form of recreation demands that it be easily teachable, and easy to carry out: hence the basic form of the step, and the simplicity of the early country-dances. The steps must be fixed, the order in which they appear must not vary too much, the tunes to which they are danced must be part of a common tradition, and insure a sufficient number of repetitions so that the pleasure need not be interrupted too often. This simple make-up of the country dances naturally left a wide margin for the inventive talent of the more skillful and enterprising in the community; the real dance-talent then came forward and invented unusual combinations, elaborated upon the steps, gave themselves up to their own creative inspiration, which was fortified by the racial inheritance and the ethnic consciousness of the group. Thus emerged the more complicated forms of folk-dancing, which, always characteristic of the nation's dance-lore, carried it up into the art-form of the National Dance. As such, National Dancing subsisted alongside the Ballet, and it is fortunate that it is still being carried in the repertoire of the ballet schools of to-day, where it serves an invaluable purpose, as a perennial fountain of freshness and inspiration. In fact, much of the best work done by the ballet schools lies in their preserving, for future generations, these treasures of the past. How much unspoiled—how long uncontaminated by the ballet practices, remains a subject for conjecture.

The common link between Folk Dancing, National Dancing, and the Ballet consists in the fact that they are reminiscent of the past, and preserve themselves by means of fixed forms, without which their integrity would soon be destroyed. Their character is determined by the exigencies of entertainment, and of communal dancing. (This holds true even of the Ballet in its original form.) Always interesting as part of the culture and civilizations of past epochs, sometimes most appealing to the æsthetic and emotional sense, they are nevertheless not expressive of the artistic consciousness of the *present*.

In this, they diverge from the Free Dance which seeks its resonance in the understanding of the present, and sends its root into the art of to-day.

It can do so only by original creation, and individual action-modes that are expressive of the inner necessity of the artist. The Free Dance can only be taught by induction and suggestion, and fostered by an organic evolution of rhythmic sensibility; whereas he Ballet, Folk and National Dancing to-day are being handed on by precept of fixed forms.

Part III

BUILDING STONES

In the Free Dance, the first attention of the trainer is concentrated on the development of the torso, as the main framework of his building. Only superficial methods of the Dance begin by fixing first the outer decorations, the movements of hands and fingers.

Following our simile of the tree, the torso appears naturally as the strong trunk from which the lighter oscillations of force flow out into the branches—here the extremities. Shake the tree, and the branches must sway too.

Thus the body swings as a whole in the Free Dance. *Impulses of action start from within the torso,* and the current is transmitted through muscular pull to the periphery, where it finds its active outlet. This projection from within the torso is not concealed, but made clearly manifest, the physical rhythm becoming the visible counterpart of the prompting current of rhythm.

The torso must be strong, and very flexible; it is easier to emit a clear kick through lever-action from the skeleton, than it is to guide the muscular action from a far point in the torso, through many avenues, to its destination on the outside. In other words, the torso has to become highly sensitized. As a general rule, the spinal column is held rather relaxed, in that readiness for action which is far from tension, because the will is suspended. The whole torso is thus held in an attitude of acute awareness. It is the central powerhouse for all action dictated to the dancer by his will or his emotions.*

* In this capacity, the torso enters almost into every action. Its function becomes apparent from the discussion of other topics in the chapters following, especially the ones on Muscular Control, Change of Weight, etc.

It is then natural that the extremities appear to be growing out of the torso in a logical continuation of its lines. They do not function separately attached to it but as the supporting roots, and the branches, grow out from a tree.*

This is most marked in the space pattern of the neo-Grecian dance forms, which changed the fifth arm position of the ballet into the "branching-out" line:

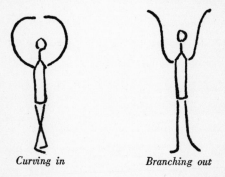

Curving in   *Branching out*

By adopting this line, the hands, turned out, instead of in, were freed for an important function: to

* Parallel with this conception goes another, quite recent development in arm movements which shows the powerful influence which the new German forms have exercised. These arm movements follow

mark the stress, or the accent, which is carried in the ballet mostly by foot action. (The foot-accent resorted to most often by the Free Dance, is stamping.)

The arms also bear most of the burden of phrasing; it is the new orientation which the arm work of the Free Dance has adopted. One hears very often that the arms carry the same function as the melody in music, and that leg motions mark the harmony. The idea is pretty, but if it were carried out meticulously, this division would result in an intolerably literal time-beating, or a "chasing of notes." However, the arms should follow, where music is used, the *phrasing* of the melody without breaking the continuity of the line, except for an occasional accent, which must be well planned. For instance, over a leg action which would carry a continuous uniform rhythm, we can imagine a steady development of the spatial arm line, spanning a sustained arch over the first phrase of the melody, then rising again in quicker action, and finishing at the end of the second phrase with a hold, an upward accent. This is the result of that kind of independent coördination which can bid two parts of the body to

the angular style and have a decided leaning towards the right angle. Modifications of this line appear in all mechanistic and "modern-istic" dancing.

[84]

execute actions on an entirely different rhythmic pattern of line, and of time.

The Free Dance does away with a fixed code of arm motions. Such a treatment of the arm work demands a good deal of the dancer. It is the fruit of much experience in arm motions, but must so sink into the unconscious mind that the dancer seems, at a given moment, quite free from any preconceived patterns, and yet commanding, from the store of his multifarious experience, such free evolutions as fit his need. Once the pattern of a composition has received its ultimate form, the arm pattern will probably not change again. In these arm motions, and the decorative touches which his hand supplies, lies the dancer's alphabet of expression.* They are his book of gestures, of air-pictures. They need not carry with them a commonly understood meaning, although such gestures as are transmitted from the past of racial consciousness, may lend great interest, if sparingly used and intelligently applied. Above all, they must be significant in some way—pictorially, musically, or

* It is a much-mooted question, whether a dancer should use much, or little, *facial expression.*

emotionally—and must never strike the literal note: except it be in a pantomimic dance.

In the Free Dance, each dancer may develop his alphabet to the point where his arm movements become a language of his own, significant of his type, or individuality. The consummation of this hope is yet to a great extent unrealized, but there is, on account of this tendency, already a bewildering wealth of spatial development in the Free Dance, which easily frightens the pupil.

A long training, and much practice is necessary, before these space patterns become second nature to the dancer. The real difficulty for the pupil, however, does not seem to lie in the amount of material which can be learned, but in the choice of his own alphabet. Which are the lines most expressive of his identity? These he ought to choose. But many never arrive at this choice; or else, they let their independence be preyed upon by considerations of fashion. Many choose in accordance with popular demands rather than with a clear insight of their mission as dancers. It is a mission that implies, first of all, the courage to be oneself, and to accept the call to expression, whether that means to show the relation to life of things grotesque and ugly, or serene and beautiful. The dancer who chases forever the "newest note," will find himself soon deprived of all individuality, hopelessly entangled in ambiguities.

And the public? Its main preoccupation at present is to appear informed of what is admissible, legitimate, and what is not. To solve this problem, it would like to have the dancers conform to a definite code. A code, even if it were feasible to lay one down amid our present diversity, would mean a death blow to the whole career of the Dance as a free development, and would lead it back to the academicism of the conventional "classic" Dance. The public must learn to suffer individuality in this as well as in other arts. There is no code for painting, sculpture; music thought it possessed one in our system of harmonies, and lo and behold! a new music has risen, likewise much to the bewilderment of the public. The only hope here as well as in other fields of art appreciation, is a patient studying, a growing along with the artists, and above all, the development of kinæsthetic feeling. That may come before another generation has found, through actual participation in the rhythmic work, a more sympathetic approach to the Free Dance. In the meantime, watching and reading can be the only means of guidance. By and by, facts and figures will sink into a few grooves of classification, and they will become more familiar, bespeaking family likeness, or contrast. However, the most stimulating experience for all those who really appreciate art, will always be the contact with a spontaneous, fresh outburst of creative exuberance. The joy of seeing genuine newness will outweigh the pleasure of recognizing some "old, familiar faces."

Possibly the most significant step which the Free Dance took in the direction of the reëstablishing lost values, was to shed the slipper. The foot was freed once more for performing fully its function, and with that, the Dance was led back to the law of its medium, and regained its natural basis.

Our concern with naturalness in art would not be justified, were it not that naturalness in many cases implies beauty. Primitive folk, in their bare feet, have a more beautiful gait than so-called civilized people possess.

Dancing must be classed as an art of the body, one which is devoted to its skill, and more particularly still, to its beauty. For centuries that other art whose main concern is likewise with the beauty of the body, —sculpture,—has glorified the human form in the nude in order to expose its lines. Shallow periods of art, that forced or tempted their sculptors to clothe their models, produced invariably mediocre results. For the Dance likewise, it cannot be the question of

[89]

more covering for the body, but only of how much more to reveal.*   Above all, it seems absurd to conceal the very part of the body which gives so much of the impetus to this art—the foot.

Does a potter cover up his hands, when he wants to mold a vase?   The very thought is ludicrous.   His art lives by the sense of touch.

Dancing, in as far as the foot is concerned, lives also by the sense of touch.   The foot is an organ of support for stationary positions; but where its function as a propelling factor comes in—and here lies, for the Dance, its main use—we must turn our attention to the laws of walking.

Walking is a changing of the weight of the body from the foot which is in the back, to the one which reaches out in front.   The body is brought forward by a push against the floor, from the toes of the back foot.   Just how well we do all this, decides the beauty of our walk; and much depends on this push-off.   In all pushing, reaching, feeling, the toes are the most efficient factors.   The bare foot gave primitive man a security in the tread which civilized man could afford

* The great interest with which nude dancing has been discussed in Europe bears witness to that argument.

to abandon in a more polished surrounding. But can a dancer give it up?

The toes secure a firm grip on the ground; with them and with the soles you can feel your way. The heavy-footed, four-legged animal does not need this sense of touch, because his eyes are reverted to the ground. Man, in his erect way of walking, has been given eyes under his feet. For the dancer to throw away this priceless gift, is folly; he needs the sense of touch on his soles, as he must use his feet with the utmost possible air of freedom.

Only in the degree that his body becomes sensitized, that all its members seem to function like beings animated with a hidden, superior intelligence, subtly aware of their surroundings, even air only: to that degree the Dance becomes telling, an enhancement of reality. The delicate way in which the toes touch the floor, or the foot is set down, or withdrawn from the floor, is of the utmost importance. The spectator must be able to follow the evolution of this movement from the very start; the toes have much to say about a dancer's intentions, about his characteristics. They should be as alive to the motion as the hands; but envelop them in so much as a flexible cloth or other covering, and they must lose the thrilling feeling of awareness to the surroundings which is so essential to an art of space. They become inert, lifeless.* A real dancer should know that he can no more cover up his most important instrument than a sculptor can go to his task with gloved hands. He would renounce some of the expression which he is striving to give through his art.

Who that has seen Botticelli's "Tobias and the Angel" would like to see the toes of these men covered up? Are they not expressive of the buoyancy of youth, of all the eagerness of expectation toward a happy end of the journey? The magnificent, rhythmic stride, the powerful forward pressing swing of these figures has, at the same time, the characteristic lightness of the unshod tread.

Botticelli's paintings alone should suffice to convert the apostles of slippered feet. If anybody yet doubts

---

* It is quite possible that some people prefer this state to the actual contact with the floor; very likely their floor is to blame for that; or else they know not the rule of sacrifice. In order to practice an art, one must give up oneself fully, without stint, not withholding anything.—Another cause for some reluctance in this respect is, that many dancers cannot afford to expose their feet. The time will come when a dancer with unsightly feet will be as impossible as one with an ill-proportioned body, and as much attention will be bestowed on the care of feet, as all civilized centuries have accorded to the hands.

that bare feet have anything expressive or beautiful in them, let them look at Flemish paintings; for instance, Roger van der Weyden's "Entombment." *

Where a painter's brush knows how to register such values on the dead canvas, is it not infinitely more important that the Dance should not lose that element of expression, which lies in the feet? Where the eye seeks for beauty, and expressiveness of the live human body as in the Dance, it must be allowed to follow the lines of the body in an unbroken current.

* Both hands and feet of the apostle John are most expressive of an all-pervading spirituality. The very quality of grief which unites all the figures on this picture in a common bond, runs from the head to the tips of those beautiful long toes, like one current drawing all the parts of the body together in an attitude of devotion and of the keenest suffering,

By listening to the laws of physical rhythm in nature as well as in the human body, the Free Dance has inaugurated an action-mode which has become the keynote of a new kinetic development. It is that technique for a slow or sudden opening up of the motion which I call the folding-unfolding type of action.

Slow motion does not always happen in the same way. For a dancer there are at least four categories, each with a different shading. In the first place, we have the well-known "slow-motion" type of the moving picture; an action, which ordinarily happens fast, is retarded on purpose, artificially. In the second place, there is the slow motion of a definitely inhibited type —as when restraint, disdain, fear, enter as determining factors; then the action works against a muscular pressure or counter-pull, and slows down accordingly. Thirdly, the almost undefinable "stealthy" type of action, which can be prompted by a great number of causes. In each of the foregoing instances, the action was retarded by some obstacle, whether actually an object placed in the way of the action, or an obstacle

[94]

built up by the will, the emotions, the imagination.

The fourth case in slow motion depends on neither of these causes. Folding-unfolding is of the very essence of the Dance, touching its core; with it, the Free Dance has happened on a finding of cosmic significance.

How do blossoms open; how do leaves unfold? A force—whose nature will remain one of the inscrutable wonders of life—presses, from a point deep within, against the limiting surroundings, presses, until the leaves give way, separate, one by one, unfold, and open to the light. The negative counterpart of the same force is the one that folded the leaves, in the first place, into the bud; the life-protecting gesture of nature which holds in a magnetic embrace all immature things.—Finally, the dried leaf drops off the tree, shriveled and exhausted. Is it the same watchful force that bids it to curl up, when at its last resting place?

Folding and unfolding is the main rhythm of all organic growth, the gentle breathing of rest and expansion, of exuberance and recoil, that goes through the universe. It is the woof and warp of nature's fabric, including our own.

When man learned to throw up his arms in sudden delight at the flush of the sun, or stretched them out in silent adoration of the starred sky—the first dance was born, cast in reverence before the unfathomable.

Up above him, the circling planets, held together in the immense fold of a magnetic force, and worlds, just tearing loose from their fiery berths, unfolded their eternal, silent Dance of Continuous Progression.

We all know who first in these modern times became aware of the tremendous portent of things like these. It was Isadora who first taught these motions full of awe-inspiring reverence, to little children. In reducing the process to a teachable technique,* we may have lost some of its inspirational quality. But

* What we retain is an unconscious seeming, but very consciously directed, action. (See also the chapter on Center of Movement, whence Folding-Unfolding emanates.) It is a slow opening-up, a lifting of the body as a whole, or in part, or of the arms only— from the Center; and a slow sinking back into a folded-in, relaxed state. This is done through the most gradual infusion of force, and gradual emptying of force, in the muscular apparatus radiating from that Center.

The same process, translated into its quick correlative, produces an outrush of force to the circumference, and a subsequent quick withdrawal; the result is a sudden radiance of motion, a flashing up of the entire being, as in moments of exuberance, in action-climax; and an equally sudden closing—the flame is drawn in, or extinct.

In the emotional strata, fear, dejection, produce folding; surprise, joy, call for unfolding. Expression Dancing draws much on the Folding-Unfolding type of action.

what was mystery yesterday becomes the knowledge of to-day. Besides, there will always be those happy few, who, piercing the veil of forms that have become habitual, will have penetrated to the core of their real significance, and know that what they practice is full of a meaning deepened by centuries. Such knowledge hallows the age-old dance forms of the Orientals. Folding-unfolding has been practiced, it would almost seem, in all eternity, anteceding any process of rational analysis. Who should be sorry that many now know what has thus been sanctioned? Here we have a technique obviously not concerned with surface values, but one of those "primary movements," which, far from being a mere imitation of nature, are yet close enough to the structural truth in nature to become an instrument of inherently rhythmic expressiveness in the service of the dancer's own vision.

The technical secret of the Folding-Unfolding action is easily revealed. It is apparent from the preceding chapters that most of the technique of the Free Dance proceeds along the avenues of muscular control.

Equal parts of relaxation and tension plus force plus intelligence, constitute the elements of muscular control. In it lies the sustaining principle which lends forcefulness and significance to motion and gesture.

All the finer instincts in human nature revolt against that which is shallow, that which has no depth beyond the surface. The appeal of the technique of muscular control—as distinct from control by the joints—is in line with that experience. The action comes from the innermost recesses of the body, it travels, as it were, a long way before it reaches the surface, and emerges there charged with all the depth of experience and force gathered along the road. It is an attack on motion prepared by long hand; let us call it the "long attack," whereas control from the joints represents the short attack. The process is a cumulative one; the action becomes expressive and significant by dint of

[98]

going to much trouble about it. The appearance of ease, however, must not be lost in the process. We know that an artist cannot cheat us by throwing easy effects upon his canvas; but on the other hand, the effort of wresting expression from a resisting medium should not appear labored.

In the same way, a dancer should know how to enhance everyday motions by calling on his resources of muscular control; but only infinite trouble will produce a really artistic counterpart. In this process, the careless, everyday step becomes an inspired processional; a hurried effort at running is transmuted into that swift streak of fluent grace which we have come to love so in Duncan-trained children.

With the secret of muscular control—although she did not speak of it in those terms—Isadora Duncan unlocked the whole gamut of natural motions. Subsequently, the manifold types of the Free Dance have applied the same key to forms of the imagination, which cover a wide range of dynamic possibilities.

The office of muscular control consists in regulating the stream of motor power by using its positive and negative tendency: relaxation and tension. They are used alternately; but the passage from one into the other show any number of shadings in between, as for instance, when a limb becomes gradually infused with force; the result is a slow lifting.

In the Free Dance, any motion becomes a matter of shadings; in the choice of those shadings, the dancer displays his intelligence and artistic taste. Muscular control equips him with this fluency of motion, the ability to take on an almost unlimited number of inflections, or shadings, for each type. For a better understanding of this diversity, it is helpful to conceive of it as of a grammar of motion, which would imply a knowledge of the following:

1. Spatial orientation:

With respect to the outlying space, a motion bears the connotations *high* or *low, straight* or *oblique, up* or *down, sideways.*

2. Physical orientation:

With respect to the body, a motion can be executed *close* to it, or away from it—*open, wide.*

3. Tensional strength:

With respect to intensity, the motion may be *strong* or *gentle, tense* or *relaxed.*

4. Time values:

With respect to the duration, the motion is *quick,*

slow, or *moderate.* (Closely related are the values: staccato-legato.)

The possible combinations across and within these four *orders of inflection* represent to the dancer what to the grammarian is his system of declensions. The command which the dancer has over them decides the richness or simplicity of his experience. This experience goes hand in hand with his mastery over muscular control. The latter commands the range of intensity, the range of (physical) distance or nearness, the spatial range; furthermore, it is within the bidding of muscular control to render the aspect of the motion simple or complex, by applying either the principle of economy or of elaboration. Control naturally implies a certain strength. To it must be added efficiency.

A person thoroughly versed in muscular control appears efficient in his movements, because he knows how to *isolate* the motion—that is, to call only on the muscles immediately necessary to the execution of that movement. This is economy, as it gives the other, unused muscles rest within the physical community, called body. Animals know this economy of movement, and that is the reason why their motions strike us as beautiful—they possess the logic of the materials with which they work, and produce the utmost possible effect with the smallest expenditure of energy. In the economy of motion lies the appeal of the so much talked-of natural movements in the Dance; the ease with which they are executed, however, results from a long study of muscular control.

Add to this process of careful selection the visible interplay of numberless smaller muscles, where the artistic aim demands it, and that may result in a heightened significance; or practice coördination of muscular control in different parts of the body, bringing them into play simultaneously, and the motion takes on an aspect of elaboration, effusion—the action-mode becomes complex.

The matter of choice in all this rests with the mind. Muscular control has its correspondence in mental selection: an agile, resilient mind alone is capable of acting in this capacity. It is the prism, through which inspiration from different sources is transformed into a light which illumines the kinæsthetic sense of the dancer, and there springs into expression.

Next to the Folding-Unfolding type of motion, and the closely related Rise-Fall motions of which we shall speak later, there is probably nothing so expressive of the new conception towards motion, than Change of Weight. With these three one could cover, if necessary, the whole range of the most *vital* action modes in the Free Dance, since the most frequently used forms would easily come under one or the other of these headings.

Change of weight is directly concerned with the problem of gravity, in which also the rise-fall motions share. The Free Dance admits weight, and thereby makes lightness more significant. We have already seen, that the Free Dance likes to face the problem of gravity in a straightforward, direct way —by accepting it as part of the law which binds the dancer into cosmic oneness with the universe around him. The problem of change of weight is of the utmost importance to the Dance, since all progression, all change of direction, all displacement, happens through a change of weight. This holds true even in the mental realm. We progress mentally, when the weight of the interest is shifted from one subject to the next. The weight of our body progresses when we move it, lift it, step by step, from one place to the next. A quickened change of weight results in a run, a leap, a skip. These are progressions in the straight line, a *change of weight back-front*.

But every *change of direction* is equally connected with a change of weight, only it then happens from side to side, from left to right. The importance of all change of direction with dancing, especially in a limited space, is evident. A swift dance covers one extension of the stage in a few seconds; having arrived at the limit of this short line, the dancer has to reverse his track, change his direction; he must *turn* in some way.

The novice, not familiar with change of weight, finds himself exceedingly embarrassed by a necessity for turning; the clumsy way by which a beginner handles this situation, the faulty foot-placing by which he tries to circumvent it, are the best evidence of the importance that should be accorded to this subject. Put on a zigzag track, he will soon find out that he is lacking some paramount knowledge, which the experienced dancer possesses. Change of weight from side to side takes the following aspects:

1. It can be an *open turn*, that is, a simple shifting of the weight of the body from the farthest side—the supporting foot—to the free foot which was in the back; and through doing so, this (formerly) free foot becomes in turn the supporting foot—the front foot in the new direction. Now the farthest foot can be picked up, and the walk, or run, or whatever movement was used, can be reversed in the opposite direction from whence it first came, until it reaches again a limit, or corner. Then the same process has to be repeated.

The open turn is then a changing of the weight of the body from one foot to the other without either of them having to be moved from the spot; there remains an opening between the knees, and the body faces the same way during the transition. But let no one think that a careless, simple shifting as we see it in everyday life, suffices here. In order to appear easy and elegant, this process must be completely translated into its dance equivalent—which requires considerable training in muscular control, balance, and an understanding of the subtle shadings inherent in change of weight. There is a change of weight *in high*, and one *in low:* slow motions do better to reverse in high (from the center of lightness), and fast motion from low (the center of heaviness in the body).

2. In connection with fast motions (like the skip), the *flinging turn* can also be employed for reversing the track. In that case, the back foot—free foot—is swung around the supporting foot, one knee crosses over the other on the way, and the swinging foot is set down in front of the first one, ready to progress in the new direction. The body has swung around 90 degrees, and is now facing in the opposite direction.

3. The *spinning turn*, in which the knees cross over each other more tightly, is a third way of changing direction. In it, the body turns completely around its axis, 360 degrees. Properly speaking, it is not a change of weight, because the very fact of it is veiled here, absorbed in fast action, so that the axis of the body remains in the same place. It belongs to the ballet equipment rather than to the Free Dance, where it is very seldom employed. The Free Dance prefers a turn not entirely in the vertical axis, which might be called the *leaning turn*, because the axis is shifted into a diagonal leaning over its base; the change of

direction is made in high, through a quick unfolding. It belongs really to the Folding-Unfolding type of action, and combines a circular change of direction with a powerful swing which brings the knees wide apart.

Change of weight finds its expression through the torso, which is thus drawn into action much more than the classical dance does. The idea of change of weight rests on a conviction that lightness and weight are both inherently necessary to movement, as the two opposite poles of the problem of progression. Progression will forever vaccilate between acceleration and retard, or rest, in proportion, as weight is taken off, or added. Nothing but a perpetuum mobile can circumvent this duality. Man has attempted to frustrate the principle of gravity in the mechanical field, but wherever he attempts it, even in the Dance, his efforts will lead him into mechanics, away from the living-reality sort of impression with which the Free Dance likes to clothe the body. There is in the Free Dance a kind of joyous acceptance of its natural lot, a grateful recognition that we possess in the body, for the best or for the worst, a marvelous instrument of expression, which is capable of endless improvement. Just in what direction improvement should be sought, that will remain subject to varying philosophical interpretations.

It is a subtle question, whether the action-modes of the Free Dance are the result of a conscious following of a certain inner logic, or whether they were evolved in an unconscious groping for expression, one element leading into the other by sheer virtue of the good rhythmic principle of a primary rhythm really strong enough to set in swing "the movements of the future in every varying natural unending sequences,"—as Isadora put it? Nobody can answer that question, at least not now; in our times,—times of multitudinous contacts and of such rapid intercourse,—nobody can fix with certainty the contribution which each individual dancer has made in the last twenty-five years, to the development of inherently free, if only incidentally new action modes.

And still, types have crystallized. Not sufficiently, however, to make the need acutely felt here for a "Grammar of Motion," such as Rudolf von Laban has offered in Germany. A premature fixing of types in the American Dance would amount to stopping short the swing of an evolution before it has become quite conscious of its own self-hood and inner necessity,

[109]

and grafting upon it a system. In order to be effective, the materials to be systematized would have to be imported along with the system; and we should have once more the absurd situation of a wholesale importation of foreign art. If art can live at all, where the talk is of systems and materials, this would be a hybrid art at its best. It seems that such an attempt at efficiency is foredoomed.

But that need not deter us from examining the powers that are at work in this new dispensation of the Dance. How does the Free Dance know its own substance, since it has abandoned the former classifications which had no bearing on a new experience?

May be few know it—it is entirely irrelevant how many, at the present moment, are conscious of any classifications. It is sufficient that there is one clearly recognizable strain which seems to have the lead in the forming of action-modes. We have come across it more than once in examining the contrast between the new and the older types of dancing, and the feeling from which the Free Dance derives and proceeds: it is that turning to physical laws of an outwardly less complicated order. Nature appears again in its age-old rôle of informer, the mirror of all known law about the visible world; the master from whom we may learn much if we do not imitate.

Since the middle of the nineteenth century, the arts have been in the process of unlearning what they knew, and the Dance is only the last comer in that line. One by one, they renounced a dogma which had laid a spell on all creative effort for centuries: the demand of objective likeness, of imitation of nature, of descriptive art in a broad sense. In that revolt, the emphasis was shifted from the object to the subject, to the artist and his vision;—and to the materials which serve as a medium of expression.

The same unremitting search for sincerity of feeling and for a representation which was appropriate to it, and at the same time truthful with respect to the medium of expression—here the body—led the Free Dance to explore and exploit for its purposes the realm of physics, but in a broader sense than heretofore.

The ballet had wrested from the body the last resistance to mechanical law. When the reaction against this attitude first set in, the motion was measured up against the human form in softer strains. In the early stages of the Free Dance, the body appeared as the representative of an intensely human being, who lived incidentally inside his body, but who had his raison d'être anyhow, independently, and apart from it. There was much talk of the soul shining through the body, the soul inhabiting it; at any rate, the soul once more took possession of the Dance, and the human emotion witnessed a glorified resurrection out of the agonizing embrace of the "frozen smile"—the only visible sign of emotion allowed during truly agonizing feats of gymnastics in which the old terpsichorean order abounded.

In the second phase * we see again the principle of distortion enter, but in a very different sense from that used before, in these acrobatic feats of the conventional dance.

Since the advent of cubism and futurism, the visual arts have used distortion, largely as a protest against what is called "photographic art"—a meticulously correct form of representation. Among other motives, distortion serves the fundamental principle of sin-

* America has only just entered on this second phase which was inaugurated in Germany more than a decade ago. However, it would be a gross mistake to believe that its main characteristic is distortion. It is mentioned here only as an old-new feature entering the arena of conflicting opinions.

cerity of expression which has become the battle cry of the artistic revolution of the twentieth century. As such—as a vehicle of sincerity—it has also its place in the Dance. If a dancer feels so, if his mind-picture presents to him objects out of the usual order, of exaggerated proportions, then he ought to present his mind-picture unalloyed, and should know the means wherewith to do so. But even in expressionistic and grotesque dancing we detect a certain cachet, a special stamp which marks the action modes as belonging inherently to the order of the Free Dance.

Throughout the Free Dance, the visual line of the action-mode is drawn somehow in closer relation to the body, than before. It remains mindful of the intensely human character which animates the body. This is a thing which only can be felt; it may be beyond explaining.

We have seen in the chapter on Comparisons how the Free Dance visualizes the body as subjected to the whole scale of physical law in its *broadest aspect*, embracing physics—gravity is there; polarity is there —and all elemental qualities and forces of nature.*

* "The Dance of the future will be a new movement, a consequence of the entire evolution which mankind has passed through." These prophetic words are from Isadora Duncan.

It represents man as in the grip of these—often conflicting—tendencies; shaken, and torn by them; or victorious in a sudden realization of harmony. The dancer appears more often led by these forces, than as a leader. He has at least renounced the rôle of self-complacent mastery.

In such a conception of nature there is no taint of imitation. From it accrues to the Free Dance a broadening, deepening influence, which acts like a filter for the thought. And by the law of like producing like, it has so happened that all the dancers who were given to such contemplation, or who somehow felt its influence, have consciously or unconsciously, evolved action-modes that have a certain family likeness to each other.

A close observer can distinguish several main types, or families, among the action-modes which the Free Dance has used in the course of its short life. It seems logical to apply to them a nomenclature which simply follows their law of derivation from the realm of physics, or from natural prototypes. Without any attempt at formal classifications which would in any sense limit the style, we can arrive at some subdivisions which might broadly serve the purpose of tracing some differentiation, and yet affording a large view.

The names here given denote only a visual impression, which anybody can easily picture for himself. Beside this somewhat dry nomenclature, it seemed only fair to point out some less obvious undertones and connotations. They may, but need not, underlie the action—for those who care to look for a deeper significance. It may afford a glimpse into the richness of a dancer's life and vision. Things like these are naturally outside of all dogma and generalizations; they are individual experiences, such as may come to a dancer who cares to listen both within and without.

Main Families of Free Action-Modes

1. The *Folding-Unfolding* type of motion should be considered in the first place, as a primary motion par excellence. It has been dealt with more fully elsewhere. Closing-opening actions belong also to this family.

2. Closely related is the family of the *rise-fall* motions, embodiment of the struggle of gravity; harkening back to the wave as their natural prototype.

3. *Press-pull* motions. In them is mirrored the duality of a universal experience—attraction-repulsion.

4. *Bending-reaching* motions—culling, cradling —the soft gestures of protective motherhood; receiving gestures; gleaning, reaping—the fullness of fruition; the wistful stretch of unappeased longing, as well as the exultance of receiving—the towering power of masculine intellect—all come to mind.

5. *Rotating and twisting; the turn.* Spirals, in which many see the birth of *all* motion, underlie this. It is the line of travail, as well as of the triumphant moments when spirit freely sheds its exuberance.

6. *Undulating and heaving.*—The eternal song of beginning and end, of rest and action. Wave-like motions translate the gentle pulse of life. The stronger motions of heaving scale all the heights of tempestuous passion, plumb the depths of despair and revolt.

7. *Swinging.*—The pendulum in motion, confined to one plane; the plaything of gravity, the eternal come and go, a symbol of conditioned freedom, of joyousness in spite of limitations. The connecting of two wave-crests, the smile from wave to wave.

8. *Swaying.*—An irregular swing, a motion through several planes. The symbol of hesitation, uncertainty—a drifting in the embrace of circumstance. Its natural prototype is the tree rooted to the spot, but sensitive to the surrounding elements.

9. *Vibrating and shaking.*—The finest shades of vibration and the last oscillations of the wave are one. Sparingly used, they become effective accents.—The stronger inflections of shaking are expressive of big elemental uprisings, and of happenings in the primitive strata of racial consciousness.*

These motions take in the body as a whole; they are big, thorough-going motions. The innumerable smaller motions, belonging to some particular part of the body—the hand, the head—have been left out purposely, as localized motions. Nor can such a general nomenclature ever attempt to register *all possible* motions, since their number is legion.

---

* In our age, an indication of the jungle. An importation of negroid character, vibrating-shaking motions have, curiously enough, been accepted as an art form of the Dance in Europe, whereas they have been confined to jazz dancing in America, so far.

"Art has all but died of good taste," Sheldon Cheney sadly remarks with regard to the visual arts in the last few centuries. The remark is directed at the excess of emphasis on representative form—the mania of correct reproduction.

It would seem that the conventional Dance has all but died of good form—divested of the ability to vibrate along with the temper of the times,—so that it eventually lost all contact with the living realities of its age.

In spite of varying fashions, there is chiseled in each solid block of time the face of the period in which art revolves. And it is art itself which wields here hammer and chisel, building this monument to time. "The signs of the times" are nothing less than a collective reflection of all that which the life of a given period meant for man, the experiences it heaped up for him. The signs of the time in which the artist lives, are usually upon his art in some undeniable fashion. With that secret mark upon it, he declares himself either in or out of harmony with the material

[118]

fabric of life surrounding him, and with the tenor of its spiritual message. Standing upon the same ground where his fellow beings stand, he shares in the common experience of life, and translates it for them as he sees it, or as he would have it be—shaping a more satisfying, immaterial experience, from the immediate materials around him.

Without partaking in some way in the spiritual experience of their times, the arts lose that resonance in the present, which echoes back from the inchoate mass of human hopes, fears, likes, dislikes, needs, and assertions; from their environment, in short. An art, which remains forever anchored in the conventions of the past, playing safe with respect to well established values, loses part of its mission. Its overtones and undertones will not be heard except by the erudite; instead of interpreting life to the onlooker, that art has to be interpreted for him.

Retrospective art invites us into the ancestral gallery of our racial inheritance. Such visits are invariably instructive; and on most occasions, delightful; but man is so constructed, that he is rooted in the present for the best or for the worst. His foremost concern is legitimately with the present; he would like to believe something good about that present; or else know how his future can be improved on. Sometimes the best lessons come from the past with respect to this last question. But—if art has any message at all—might he not expect that such a word of enlightenment, such a sudden radiance about the present, or a vision of the future,—should be opened up to him by the artists, those fellow beings supposedly endowed with an acuter vision, a keener perception of values, than the ordinary man? If the artist creates not only for his own enjoyment, but to make himself articulate to the world—and artists are generally credited with that desire—then such a conception of the mission of art has nothing uncommon about it.

Art can speak to us comfortingly, illuminatingly, wittily, ironically, sympathetically, or hopefully, as the case might be, about this present or the future world. If an artist cannot at all tune in with the present, the fault may be with him as much as with that present; but there are few artists who, seeking persistently the escape into a more beautiful and perfect past, have been able to capture the imagination of their fellow beings for any length of time. A continued borrowing of past action-modes and models

[120]

is a tacit admission that the source of inspiration—
creative genius—runs but shallow.

Should this effort at interpreting the trend of the
present plunge us into another process of photographic
reproductions? What else, but disaster could come
from it to art, in the present, rather materialistic age?
Photographic processes are always a doubtful recourse
for art. Artistic taste knows where to draw the line
which separates creation from imitation; suggestion,
illusion, from stark reality. After all, an age is rep-
resented as much in its reflexes, in all the emotional
reactions which have set in over it and against it, than
in its *realistic forms and outer movement.* Is the
object of art our machine age, or man as moved by it?
If art should busy itself with the latter problem, it
will become soon apparent that man's inner mechanism is now more flexible, capable of more inflections
than he ever possessed before; and again, that man
is the same man, only multiplied, as it were; heir to
millions of men gone before him in the much-lamented
past.

Man is then more mobile than before.—One more
important change: he passes more quickly from one
stage to the other. The pulse of life has quickened

for him—his rhythm is not only more varied, but faster than before. He no longer consents forever to weep, forever smile, forever enthuse, forever groan: weeping, smiling, exulting, suffering, become inflections of the eternal theme of life, punctuated by stops, pauses, recuperation; and the rhythm of the present moves swiftly on, over more and more complex obstacles, touching again and again the low points of despair and tragedy, the high points of revolt and victory.

Here, what an age for the Dance! Shall we spend it all in remembering the past? Or shall we not rather take up the new possibilities of our present experiences which press upon us from all sides, and clothe them with the idealism of good hope?

It is pleasant to dream about the past, but to be equal to the present is more. The Free Dance has much to learn from the past, but it is not willing to perpetuate it. The real task is to interpret the present, and sense the future. To be equal to it, taste—much taste!—will be necessary. A dancer nowadays must have in his education an unfailing compass to tell him where to go. He can ill afford to despise the varied sources of education—especially art-literature in its most telling aspects—if he would sharpen his faculties of right choice. Unless he is a genius such as few are, he will lose his way in his own art without an intimate acquaintance with the other arts, with music, and with philosophy. A genius educates himself; talent needs guidance.

Education, appreciation, philosophy: around these valuable possessions of an intellectual kind, the invisible hedge of humility should be early drawn. A deep humility, which will prevent these prerequisites (which are, after all, only tools with which to dig at the real treasure) from becoming too apparent. Humility of the most impersonal kind alone will enable the dancer to know how to yield, and so get access to those depths whence effortless, the stream of rhythmic experience rises and breaks into dancing. Taste must see to it that this rising stream is kept clear of the willful flood of the ego, which does more than any other element to destroy the dancer's form.

After all, it is creative joy, rhythmic sensibility and technical fitness, which constitute the real dancer. Let us suppose he has these precious gifts. What will he do with them?

The dancer's first task is to establish a right balance between these three. Balance appears in the first stage of the dancer's experience as courage. Uncomprehending, but courageous, he throws himself into the

[124]

motion and is happy when it carries him, much as the water carries the swimmer. A little later he will know that it *must* carry him. That is the moment when he becomes first aware of the laws of physical balance. A right physical balance is attained when courage and intelligence unite the results of the physical advance with the growth of understanding which has taken place during the training period. These two do not always keep step with each other. One dancer may proceed faster along the road of physical development, another along the mental. But the dancer cannot attain real mastery in spatial balance before the results of both are equal.

In the second stage, balance takes on an entirely different meaning. It appears then as an understanding of harmonious proportions in general; in particular, as a study of the problem of attraction and repulsion. From a viewpoint of higher philosophical conception, the dancer contemplates balance as holding the immovable post between those two principles of dynamic force.

Both balance and harmony are "dwellers in the secret place of the most high." Fortunately or unfortunately, there is not much that can be taught

[125]

about them by precept. They will probably forever remain the coveted possession of innate talent.

Harmony has been variously defined as the concord of the component parts of a whole, or as an affinity between various sequences of the same structure. The simplest use of harmony is symmetry. In Greek, the two words harmony and balance were at times almost identical; to harmonize could mean to balance component parts, to fasten a keystone into a structure. Together, balance and harmony erect the superstructure also over the Dance, after all the other requirements are fulfilled.

This superstructure is both exclusive of much—shallowness, ignorance, and empty imitation—and inclusive of all that is endowed with real creative force. In this latter sense, it is a true superstructure. Under its protective roof distinctions become null; it can shelter all types of the creative Dance,—with music or without. Distinctions of style vanish, where perfection of artistic conception enters.

Harmony may be likened to a perfume distilled from many flowers of perfection; as alluring, and intangible as a perfume; whilst balance is the secret of mixing these ingredients in the right proportion.

Change these harmonious proportions, and the result is a disastrous discord.

Balance appears in the right distribution of the elements belonging to a dance composition. Such distribution bespeaks the individuality of the dancer, not only in the way he handles these single elements, —movement, rest, force, feeling, intensity, line,— but also in his preference for one or the other. A dancer may stress one element, particularly, but his feeling for balance will tell him just how far he may go with his preference without disturbing the harmony of the whole. And so balance and harmony will forever appear together, linked in purpose, making for unity of impression.

After having attained this second stage of balance, the dancer is ready for his task. He stands, listening. On the one hand, is his audience; on the other, his inner necessity, the visible world around him, the invisible world beyond him: these three are the music to which he dances. Now he will so establish himself between his audience and his music, as to become the interpreter from one to the other, distilling from the visible world around him the finest values, and re-translating them into visibility through motion, which appears charged with the meaning of his own vision. Or, he may take his flight into the invisible world, and transform for his audience its four-dimensional qualities into three dimensions—its spiritual message into a living experience.

The three dimensions in which the dancer works are space, time, and thought,—an infinite, limitless realm. Being in tune with the infinite is to feel harmony. With this conception in mind, can the dancer seek for values by precept and aim at mechanizing his motion?—The question seems futile. He uses the Free Dance as the instrument which will give the fullest and the freest scope to his expression. It enables him to become the most direct interpreter of the stress and the joy of the present, the beauty and the tenderness of the past, the promise and the visions of the future—in those supreme moments when he attains a full realization of harmony.

Part IV

APPENDIX

LINEAR RHYTHM The dynamic Rhythm, or Rhythm of movement, has its spatial correspondence in *linear rhythm*, each movement describing in its evolution certain traceable paths in space.

We have to distinguish:

1. The *track* or floor pattern, which the dancer's feet trace on the floor.

2. The *space pattern*, which is traced by the extremities, or by the whole body, *in the air;* lines of movement that may briefly touch the ground but are mostly written into space, much like the aviator's "sky-writing."

3. *Spatial composition*, or the way in which the choreograph (be he identical with the dancer, or a person planning the evolution of an entire dancing chorus) fills the space available to him; always bearing in mind the relation of all these movements or moving bodies en masse, to the *three-dimensional qualities of the stage.* This is a study in itself, and belongs properly in the field of composition.

The daily routine of the dancing student involves constant use of linear rhythms, and it is essential that the feeling for track and space pattern particularly, become for him an ever-present reality. The properties of spatial composition are for the present hardly a teachable subject, and will remain for some time a field open for exploration to a chosen few who possess a special talent in that direction. Therefore space composition is a topic with which the student will hardly burden himself, but he will be an appreciated member in any chorus which such an expert choreograph may direct, as long as he is at least well versed in track and space patterns.

A clear conception of track and space patterns adds precision and elegance to a dancer's technique, and he will advance much more rapidly if he is able to hold his attention constantly to these linear rhythms. This requires a good deal of visual memory. The linear rhythms become for him, so to speak, invisible roads in space; lines which he traces, after technique has enabled him to command the necessary muscular control, with as much certainty into space as a bird, who, darting through the air, is not only moved by accident, but by a decided will towards certain directions. In fact, the dancer will approach the wonderful sensation of flying, which he shares with birds, in the measure as his work loses the character of accidental movement—falling, tripping, wavering—with its heaviness, and becomes instead directed dynamics.

FLOOR TRACK   It helps the vividness of impression upon the memory to trace the paths of linear rhythm, which express, as it were, the edge of dynamic motion.

The track on the floor is easiest to reconstruct. Be it in walking, running, leaping, or turning, the dancer's feet move along the floor in certain directions of which he is conscious as an uninterrupted pattern. (See page 134 for some examples.) The line connecting all those points constitutes the floor track.

It is of great importance, especially in a chorus, that every member should trace the floor pattern, which is then common to all, with absolute exactness. The floor pattern played a great part in folk dancing, as, for instance, in Morris Dances. Even in the earlier stages of the ballet, when folk dancing was bent to court use, all attention seemed to be concentrated on elaborate floor patterns; but when the space pattern, or the evolution of arms and legs in space, began to receive the same care, the ballet definitely outgrew the limits of folk dancing and became an art form. It remained for the twentieth century to add to this two-dimensional orientation of the Dance the concern and the feeling for the three-dimensional, outlying space.*

* This problem has received special attention from some masters of choreography in Germany and Russia.

A FEW BASIC TYPES OF TRACK

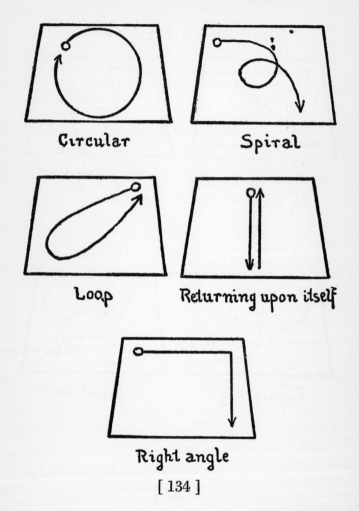

Circular

Spiral

Loop

Returning upon itself

Right angle

[134]

A FEW BASIC TYPES OF TRACK

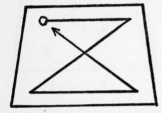

Straight lines conn.
by diagonals

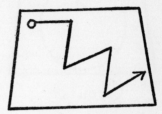

Zig-zag line

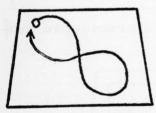

Figure eight

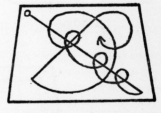

Combination

SPACE PATTERNS Space patterns can be traced by any part of the body, but for the purposes of the Dance the space patterns of arms and legs are the most important. This does not mean that the dancer can, or should, restrict himself to the movements of arms and legs; on the contrary, most of these movements are directed in the Free Dance from the torso as their source of dynamic rhythm. However, this dynamic force finds its strongest *visible* echo in the linear rhythm of the extremities which utilize the original impetus, coming from the torso, in a manifold way. Whereas the linear activities of the best trained torso are limited to a comparatively few possibilities outside of bending, stretching, circling, and twisting, the graphic presentation of the other space patterns show infinitely more variety.

The path of the movements describes the following lines in space:

1. Straight lines, moving forward and back, or up and down, on the same track. They are bi-polar motions; returning upon themselves, plying between two opposite poles, from starting point to end point, and back again. Example: Rise-fall motions, pushing-pulling, extending-withdrawing. They may lie in any plane.

2. Wave lines. The dynamic action here corresponds to an extending-withdrawing of the arms within two parallel horizontal (less frequently vertical) planes.

3. Circles, and half-circles, lying in one plane. Example: Front arm circles.

4. Loops. Example: Arm swing from center front (cf) to right high one (1rh).*

* See page 140 in *Planes*.

[136]

5. The figure 8, in all planes.

6. The spiral, or a series of circling movements through several parallel planes.

Besides, there is the possibility of any number of combinations of these lines, as well as the varied field of geometrical angles.

Some of the leg movements partake of the floor track, as the walking step; the running step (farther apart); the leap (still farther apart), and the skip (hop-step with elevation). Free in the air are again the swinging movements, loops, half-circles, and angles.

PLANES A clear conception of direction or *planes,* is indispensable to the correct execution of space patterns. Since space patterns cannot all lie in one plane, as the floor track, it is not possible to render the space pattern adequately with one line, unless the angle in which this particular plane lies with respect to the floor, is perfectly clear. For purposes of a simple orientation it is best to know first definitely the three main planes, although the action-modes in the Free Dance, which is especially rich in transitions, touch innumerable planes, and cannot be circumscribed by these three only.

1. *The vertical plane* connects all points lying straight across the body in the direction from hip to hip and shoulder to shoulder. To it belong all movements executed in this plane. Example: Lifting of arms overhead.

2. *The horizontal plane* is imagined as laid through the center of the body parallel to the floor,—at about the height of the hips,—dividing it into an upper and a lower half. To it belong all movements lying in it or parallel to it, such as leg circles, or floating motions of outstretched arms, head circling, etc.

3. *The back-forward plane* can be imagined as dividing the body exactly into a right half and a left half. To it belong all movements which lie in back-forward direction with respect to the front of the body. Example: Leg swing forward and back.

These three planes cut each other at right angles. It is, of course, impossible to cover with them the endless number of movements which can be executed by the extremities. This would require an intricate graphic scheme with a great

[138]

many planes at tilted angles.* Without going to complicated schemes—which constitute a science more interesting
than immediately helpful to the Dance—the dancer will do
well to fix in his consciousness some minimum requirement
of linear orientation by means of the three fundamental
planes. They, with their easily remembered parallel planes,
will cover a good deal.

In addition, we can identify a great number of points in
the following way:

By calling all points in front of first plane, *front;* all
points lying in the back of first plane, *back.*

By calling all points above second plane, *high;* all
points below, *low.*

By calling all points to the right of third plane, *right;*
all points lying to the left, *left.*

We gain thus on the right side of the body: Points high
(h), low (lo), front (f), back (b). On the left equally:
Points h, lo, f, b.

These points allow for many combinations, and can
serve to name the starting point and the end point of any
movement in space. For instance:

r h f	l h f
r h b	l h b
r lo f	l lo f
r lo b	l lo b

indicate points which lie *parallel* to the three planes.
Points lying right *in* the different planes might be called:

* Such as Rudolf von Laban's Icosaëder.

In the first (vertical) plane:

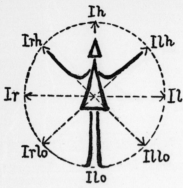

Vertical Plane

1 l
1 r
1 r h
1 r lo
1 l h
1 l lo
1 h
1 lo

1 h is the point lying straight overhead.
1 lo is the floor point of the body axis.

In second (horizontal) plane:

2 r

2 l

2 f

2 b

2 r f

2 l f

2 r b

2 l b

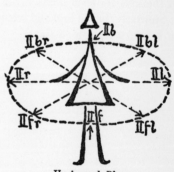

Horizontal Plane

In third (back-forward) plane:

3 f h

3 f lo

3 b lo

3 b h

3 h

3 lo

3 f

3 b

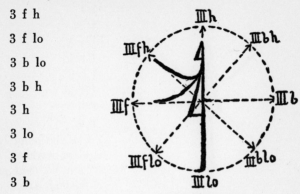

Back-Forward Plane

1 high and 3 high, 1 low and 3 low, are identical points; since the first and third plane intersect at right angles, their axis is identical, and so are the two opposite points of the axis for each plane.

Similarly, in the first and second plane, 2 left corresponds to 1 left, 2 right to 1 right.

PART V

GLOSSARY OF TERMS

GLOSSARY OF TERMS

The technical terms used in connection with the Free Dance vary in meaning according to individual interpretation. In this Glossary (which is meant to help the lay reader to a fuller understanding of this highly controversial subject) the first paragraph after each word gives its most commonly understood meaning, while the second paragraph gives the author's own interpretation, suggestion or comment.

The expressions marked with an asterisk are terms which, to the author's knowledge, have not been so used before, with reference to the Dance. Their introduction became necessary in order to designate a meaning for which terms have been lacking.

ABSOLUTE DANCE: Used in Germany to designate the new phase of the Dance that lays the main emphasis on dynamic rhythm. This tendency claims for the Dance the same independence as all other arts have, in the consciousness of their inherent selfhood and uniqueness; it needs no music, resting on its own laws.—Used as a synonym for: The Dance without music. (See "Unaccompanied Dance."

ACCENT: Stress.
An accent in the dance is that sudden intensifying of a motion—often done by deviating from the previous

course—which marks a certain moment as significant within the general flow of action and rhythm. It can occur almost anywhere—usually coincides with the musical accent—most often at the start, the climax, or the end of a phrase. The accent may also be brought in direct opposition to the musical accent, as counterpoint. There is an upward and a downward accent in the Dance.

ACROBATIC DANCING: A form of dancing that abounds in acrobatic feats, in bending and flexing the body beyond all natural proportions.

*ACTION-MODE: With this term I mean to designate types of movement in the Free Dance. Since the division into foot-work and arm-work is not so clearly marked here as in the Ballet, the word "steps" is not properly descriptive of the movements in the Free Dance. They are mostly through-going, using the whole body at once. "Action-modes" might then be taken as a collective term for such sequential dynamic action as the Free Dance employs in its combinations of leg motion, arm gesture, and torso-work.

ÆSTHETIC DANCING: A simplified type of ballet, employing the five "standard positions" (but not insisting on turning out the foot fully ninety degrees) and ballet "steps" and combinations, besides conventional arm gestures.

A misnomer, which deserves to be discarded, because it leads to much confusion. People who are not familiar with any more specific classifications, like to supply it promiscuously to all types of dancing which are not deemed unæsthetic by them. "Æsthetic Dancing" practices a superannuated æstheticism without idea or expression, and attempts neither the solid accomplishment of the ballet, nor the sincere expression of the Free Dance; although it will sometimes take off the ballet slippers and appear barefooted.

AMATEUR: Current meaning: a dabbler in art.

Here used in its original meaning: one who loves the occupation with some art, without being a professional.

*APPLIED DANCE: The Dance as applied to some occasion outside of its foremost sphere; in contrast to the non-illustrative dance.—Much dancing is done in the service of other arts and of different causes. In that case the dance is conditioned by the occasion which demands its coöperation. It is then not independent, but governed by some laws which lie outside of its own selfhood, and often becomes illustrative, or story-telling. The dance-drama, dramatic chorus dancing, dancing in pageantry, pantomimic dancing, personification, character dancing, the common type of dramatic dancing which enacts happenings—all belong to the Applied Dance.

ART-DANCE: A type of dancing whose aims are in alignment with the general aims of art.—

An expression evidently devised to avoid identification with those forms of the Dance that aim at mere accomplishment, entertainment, or a shallow sort of æstheticism. It began to be used here in the earlier stages of the Free Dance, but never came into general use, probably for euphonious reasons, and the expression "serious dancing" is now sometimes substituted for it. Obviously, "serious dancing" does not connote the same thing, though, for art is not always seriously minded. A correct, qualifying term seems almost an essential to any discussion of the modern Dance. The need has been felt everywhere with the advent of a renaissance of the Dance, and most European languages possess an equivalent of "Art Dance" or "The Dance as an Art." In Germany, where the literature on the Free Dance is most diffuse, both terms have been accepted long ago and are being used interchangeably.

ARTICULATIONS: Joints.

ATTITUDES: A term of the ballet, denoting standing positions in strictly prescribed form, where both feet rest on the floor.

AXIS: The straight line around which something rotates or turns.

GLOSSARY OF TERMS

BALLET:

    1. A complete pantomime or play in which a story is told, and actions, characters and passions are shown by gestures, accompanied by music and dancing.

    2. The company or persons who perform the dance or the play.   *—Winston's Simplified Dictionary*

    The origin of the ballet goes back to 1489, when this mixed form of opera, dance, and pantomime was first introduced in a sumptuous festivity at the court of the Duke of Milan. This type of spectacle traveled afterwards from court to court all through the European countries, but received its most significant development in the French Court of Louis XIV. The birthday of the ballet is sometimes set at 1581, the date when Baltazarini produced his famous "Ballet comique de la reine" at the Court of Henry the Third and Catharine de Medici.—

    The ballet to-day appears as a form of dancing which teaches by means of fixed rules a technique of the Dance that presumably covers all needs of any dancer.

CHANGE OF WEIGHT: The shifting of the body-weight from one foot to the other through dance-motion.

CHARACTER DANCE: A dance in which a certain character is portrayed; for instance, Pierrot, Columbine, etc.

CHOREGRAPHY: A system of describing all the movements of a dance by means of signs and symbols. Sev-

[149]

eral such systems have been used in connection with the ballet. (For instance, Zorn's.)

Synonym for Dance-script. (See *ibid.*)

CHOREOGRAPH: One who invents or designs the dances for a chorus.

Choreography: the design or composition of a choral dance. (Should not be confounded with choregraphy.)

CLASSIC DANCE: Used in two ways:

1. To denote the conventional ballet. Classic training means a training in the formal ballet style.

2. Less frequently, it is applied to the classic Greek style.

CONSONANCE: In music, agreement of sound.—Harmony.

*CONVENTIONAL DANCE: Such types of dancing as proceed through motions fixed by convention or tradition. The Folk Dance, the National Dance, and the Ballet; to an extent, also, Character Dancing would come under this heading.

CORPS DE BALLET: The dancers engaged in producing a ballet.

CRESCENDO: In music, a gradual increase in sound. In the Dance, a gradual increase in force of dynamic action, or expression.

DANCE-AS-AN-ART: Synonym for Art Dance. (See *ibid.*)

DANCE-SCRIPT: A system of notation for the Dance, whereby the dynamic and spatial development of a dance are exactly described. Recently, Rudolf von Laban has published the results of ten years of study in this field. He has devised a complete new dance-script, resembling more the system of musical notation than the ancient systems of choregraphy. It can be used on note-paper, the signs employed—mostly dashes and dots—lying horizontally along the lines and between the intervals.

DECRESCENDO: In music, a gradual diminishing of sound. In the Dance, a gradual restriction of the force of motion, or expression.

DISSONANCE: In music, disagreement of sound.—In general, discord.

DIVERTISSEMENT: Entertainment. In the ballet, the portion of a program—usually at the end—which brings a series of shorter, varied, and light numbers.

*DOWN-STROKE: Corresponding, in music, to the beat which gets the heavy accent. In the Dance, it may be taken in its literal sense: a downward motion. When translating the musical *accent*, however, the dynamic accent in the dance can point up, as well as down.

DYNAMIC: Pertaining to power, or to forces producing motion. It is used in this latter sense (with respect to the Dance) in this book. For definition of Dynamic Rhythm, see page 36.

*ENERGIZED ACTION: Dance-Motions freely fed by the dynamic stream of energy; the opposite of what I call Passive Action. (See *ibid.*)

EN MASSE: In great numbers. Used in chorus dancing.

EXPRESSION DANCING: The term is self-explanatory: a type of dancing where the aim is expression.—The term is not as widely used as it deserves. No other term, however, is so immediately expressive of the aim of the Free Dance. With expression as the aim, form and rhythm as the means, the task of the Free Dance is succinctly described. Expression dancing can present a wide range of possibilities: mood, rhythmic interpretations, abstract ideas, dramatic feeling,—and thus becomes a rather inclusive term.

EXPRESSIONISTIC DANCING: A form of dancing allied in spirit to what is called expressionism in the static arts.

The meaning of this term is by no means settled.—In Germany, where Expressionism has had its fullest swing, it is generally understood as stressing the values of the inner reality rather than the outer appearance of the subject; accordingly, expressionism uses any technique or method adequate to emphasize that deeper structural character, and is not concerned with surface likeness nor accepted æsthetic standards.

The term has appeared here very recently, and has been very loosely applied (with respect to the Dance). It is sometimes connected with dancing of an exaggerated, or distortionist nature, or to denote any somewhat unusual type of dancing. By such a use, attention is hardly directed to Expressionism, but to the difficulty of deciding where art ends and where exaggeration begins.

FLOOR PATTERN: The design which the dancer's feet trace on the floor in the process of his dance. Synonym for: Floor-Track.

FOLDING: In the Dance, a slow sinking of the body in its vertical axis, when energy is gradually withdrawn from the five main articulations where folding is possible.— A closing, drooping of the body.—Some systems understand this term as a gradual return from the upright vertical position to a horizontal position on the floor. The method employed is always relaxation.

ELEMENTS OF THE FREE DANCE

Forte: A term in music, meaning strong, loud. In the Dance, energized motion.

*Free Dance: With this term I mean to designate all types of dancing that have sprung up as a consequence of the free evolution which the Dance took since Isadora Duncan's pioneering work encouraged the breaking away from the traditional dance with its fixed forms (see Chapter Free Dance *versus* Fixed Forms). The earmarks of the Free Dance at its best—in the art forms—are: Freely evolved action-modes, rhythmic sensibility, the rhythmic attack on motion, creative thought, genuine feeling, and original composition work which rests on an understanding of the artistic temper of our age. It appears almost invariably as barefoot work.—There are in the Free Dance probably as many varieties as there are truly creative artists who have adopted it; besides untold less successful or mistaken attempts as they occur in any field of art. Some types are patterned more or less closely after the Duncan style. Other types are as far removed as can be from the earlier, neo-Grecian forms which this striving after a Free Dance took at first. Since the War, probably as a result of the reopening of international relations in art, there has been a wholesome tendency to more diversification and originality in style and thought. Thus we see on the opposite pole from the neo-Grecian style, such exhibitions of dancing as Expressionism and the many varieties of Interpretative and Expression Dancing,—all are certainly types of Free Dancing.

[154]

FREE FOOT: In the Dance, the foot which does not support the body-weight, and is therefore free to carry the next action.—The opposite: Supporting Foot (see *ibid*).

GREEK SCHOOL: That school of the Dance which follows Greek modes—the chief models being Greek vase paintings. (See Neo-Grecian dance form.)

HEALTH DANCING: Dancing used as a health-giving exercise and applied to hygienic purposes.

ICOSAEDER: An icosahedron, or solid of twenty equal sides or faces. Rudolf von Laban used this geometric device to make clear his spatial orientation in a system of sequential arm work.

IMPULSE, IMPETUS: The propelling tendency of a force, which will spend itself in some action along the way.

INTERPRETATIVE DANCING: (Shortened by many to "interpretive" dancing.)

A type of dancing where impression precedes expression, and the idea dictates form and means.

As the earliest—and still very diffuse—type of the

Free Dance, Interpretative Dancing means for most people a visual interpretation of music through the Dance. This practice is age-old, but the new name given to it seems to have aroused considerable opposition among musicians, who contend that music needs no interpretation. But the interpretative dancer does not say that music needs him; rather, that he needs music because it tunes his being, so to speak, for his task, by virtue of that secret undercurrent of rhythm and mood which the two arts have undoubtedly in common. It is true that the mistaken efforts of many dancers who approached their "interpretations" without any knowledge of music, seem to have justified the protests of the opponents.

Interpretative Dancing at its best is a non-illustrative type of dancing. It must combine a keen sense of analysis pertaining to music composition, with fine rhythmic sensibility, and an imaginative concept of dance form. Thus the structure of music can be translated into a three-dimensional space composition, and a new creation arises, the spirit of music as seen and felt by the dancer.

In a broader sense of the word, almost all recital dancing of the Free type is interpretative, where it is not character work. No matter what method the dancer uses, as long as he expresses his inner vision, he is about to *interpret*, by means of silent motion, his mood, or his idea. In this form, Interpretative Dancing is almost identical with Expression Dancing. (This more recent term may supplant by and by the older one.) Together, these two types have done most to establish the Free Dance as an art-form on the stage.

KINÆSTHETICS: The sense of muscular effort.

Kinæsthetic sensation: the sensation which informs us of bodily movement.

LEGATO: A term in music, derived from "legare," to bind. In the Dance, connected motions.

MODERNISTIC DANCE: A vague term, used alternately with Expressionistic Dancing. Both expressions are obviously endeavoring to point at a type of Free Dance which is not allied to the neo-Grecian movement, using radically different action-modes.

MECHANISTIC DANCE: A dance which is reminiscent of the machine, of artificial mechanisms. The motions are mechanical, jerky, and mostly angular.

NATURAL DANCING: Variously defined as a method used in educational work, placing less emphasis on form than on expression. The objective is to develop a vigorous, controlled and expressive body through the most efficient use of natural movements.

A broad term which has survived from the times of the first reaction against the formal and stilted type of the old Ballet. All exponents of natural dancing are agreed that they use "natural motions" and that they seek for self-expression. Whereas no succinct definition of Natural Dancing has been put forth, one writer enumerates the "natural movements" used in her system as: walking, running, skipping, leaping, whirling, galloping, stretching, bending, jumping, throwing, grasping, turning, and relaxation (?).—Natural dancing is much used for corrective purposes, and appears sometimes as "Health Dancing."

NATURE DANCING: A form of the dance whose concern is presumably with the life of nature.

Under this name the conventional dancing schools teach a story-telling type of dancing of the most vapid sort; catching butterflies, picking flowers, etc. Some barefoot schools have used it as an escape from self-consciousness, only to fall into sentimentality. Nature Dancing serves a useful aim in so-called educational dancing, and has its place in the teaching of children and in pageantry.—Abroad the term is unknown, and it is foredoomed to disappear here as a relic of photographic art.

*NEO-GRECIAN DANCE FORM: A new adaptation of what is known about the dancing of the ancient Greeks.

In view of the great uncertainty attached to all emulation of Greek dancing, I prefer to speak of these efforts as the neo-Grecian dance form. Attention was first directed toward Greek action-modes through Delsarte's mirror of gesture which was based on the study of Greek statuary. It remained for Isadora Duncan to discover the use of Greek principles of harmony as applied to actual *through-going dance form*. There seemed to be a fruitful field of exploration, and the promise of a tangible form induced numberless schools of dancing and of rhythmic expression to exploit Grecian prototypes, as a near-ideal, in the general search for more freedom of expression. The pitfalls of adaptation and imitation became soon apparent, and Isadora herself persistently disclaimed any intention of imitating Greek dancing, and any connection with these so-called followers. However, the use of Greek principles of balance and of body-action could not but result, and will always result, in a dance form which is near-Grecian in character, although it may be filled with a modern spirit. The neo-Grecian School, scorned by many now, has nevertheless done the pioneering for the Free Dance. It supplied, if not the form, at least some of the basic principles on which the Free Dance proceeded: *the necessity of impression preceding expression, the unity of action and meaning, and the secret of through-going motion.*

NEW DANCE: A new dispensation of the dance, different from the conventional dance forms. (See *ibid.*)

The term has been largely used in central Europe to designate the new German mode of dancing which proclaimed its independence from music and evolved radically new action-modes (see Foreword). In America, it is often used as a synonym of what I call the Free Dance, which is, however, a more inclusive term than New Dance.

* NON-ILLUSTRATIVE DANCE: The dance *per se;* the opposite of what I call the Applied or Illustrative Dance. (See *ibid.*)

[159]

The Non-Illustrative Dance exists for its own sake; it depends on no other necessity but that of expressing the inner necessity of the dancer, and follows no other laws but those inherent in its nature as a self-sufficient and unique art form.

PADDING: In the dance, the filling in with sundry motions (mostly in moments of transition), which are obviously an outcome of embarrassment and have no relation to the main stream of dynamic rhythm.

*PASSIVE ACTION: Dance action carried out with relaxed muscular control. The dancer seems passive, drifting with the impulse of some rhythm. (See chapter on Emotional Rhythm.)

PHRASE: In music: a group of notes representing a musical idea.

In the Dance, the phrase consists of a series of movements which are bound together by a logical rhythmic development. Its duration should coincide with the musical phrase, where music is being used.

PSEUDO-GREEK: That which attempts to be Grecian in aspect, and is not. Much of the dancing heralded as "Greek," especially in the commercial schools, is only pseudo-Greek, make-believe, because divested of that basic knowledge and the taste which are necessary for a plausible rendering of Grecian dance modes.

RALLENTANDO: A term in music, derived from rallentare, to slow down. It means the same thing in the Dance.

RHYTHMIC DANCE: A method of bringing out the rhythmic quality in dancing.

Whether the emphasis is placed on musical correlation (this seems to prevail in America) or on the varieties of rhythmic impulse (as in central Europe), Rhythmic Dancing stresses rhythmic sensibility as the end, and uses muscular control as the means. The forms differ widely. Most of the art forms of the Free Dance find their expression through one of the many varieties of rhythmic dancing, which thus appears as a technique, a means to an end of expression. It also serves a widespread need in educational work.

I see in Rhythmic Dancing an effort at bringing the interest for natural movements into systematic channels. It is always coupled with an informed and responsive attitude towards music, and works for more or less definite results in æsthetic form without sacrificing the sincerity of expression.

RHYTHMIC SENSIBILITY: The quality of being sensitive to rhythm; sensing rhythmic developments and possibilities.

ELEMENTS OF THE FREE DANCE

*SPACE PATTERN: The pattern which the dancer traces into space by his evolutions, chiefly through arm work.

*SPATIAL COMPOSITION: A type of dance composition which proceeds from a definite feeling for the three-dimensional enclosure of the stage on which the dancer works. Its spatial values are used so as to become a part of the artistic impression which the dancer wants to create for his audience.

STACCATO: A term in music, derived from staccare, to disconnect. In the Dance, disconnected motion.

STEPS: A term of the conventional dance, denoting fixed forms of dancing motions. The ballet, folk and national dancing are based on steps, or "pas," as the French expression runs.

SUPPORTING FOOT: In the dance, the foot which supports the weight of the body. It is an accepted principle in dancing that a person needs only one foot to stand on, the whole weight of the body resting on that foot.

TRACK: Synonym for: floor pattern. (See *ibid.*)

UNACCOMPANIED DANCE: Dancing without any musical accompaniment.

162

Rudolf von Laban and Mary Wigman first developed this form of the dance, which has been much used in central Europe. (My article, "The New German Credo," in the New York *Evening Post* of Jan. 12, 1929, treats this subject at some length.) Sometimes percussion instruments, like the drum or tom-tom are being used to mark or to accentuate the rhythm but no musical theme underlies the dance composition, which follows an independent rhythmic development of the dancer's own devising.

Synonyms of this term are: The Dance without music, and The Silent Dance—a less fortunate expression, since it overlooks the fact that the Dance has become nowadays definitely a silent art.

UNFOLDING: In the dance, the technique of a slow or quick opening up of the body, when the muscular pull gradually travels from the lowest point to the highest point of unfoldment. (See chapter on Folding-Unfolding.)—Some understand unfolding as a certain exercise where the body is lifted from a horizontal, prone position to the strictly vertical, standing position.

*UP-STROKE: In the Dance, an upward motion.

THE END